HINTS FOR PIANO NORMAL STUDIES

By

W. K. BRECKENRIDGE

Vantage Press, Inc., New York

CONTENTS

Preface

APPENDIX

PREFACE

The purpose of this book is to provide suggestions to young teachers of piano. It is more especially for those who, after having been graduated from a school of music, decide to teach, and find that in the stress of learning, or finishing a recital program, they have underestimated the problem involved in teaching others, and have neglected to equip themselves with an adequate teaching repertory.

The subjects have all been used for discussion and debate in class, and have been found extremely useful. No claim is made that the accompanying lists contain all that is worthwhile under their respective topics. The progressive teacher will constantly find additional material to add to them.

The primary grades have purposely been omitted as belonging to a different field.

THE AUTHOR

ON ESTIMATING THE NEW PUPIL'S NEEDS

Technique is primary—all pupils need technique. First, independence of finger and wrist, a good scale, and a good arpeggio. A light crisp touch for leggiero effects is much less likely to come than a heavy touch.

Have the pupil play something: watch his hands; observe his time and fingering. Ask him what gives him the most difficulty; what he considers his worst faults; what he likes best.

If he plays dryly and uninterestingly, it may be not entirely his fault. Perhaps he has no sense of what he is trying to do. It is of little use to tell a pupil to play with more finish, or more expressively, for he may not understand you. You must show him how, by illustration.

If he is weak in rhythm, then proceed accordingly. Give him thorough drill in all kinds of rhythms.

If he has certain special muscular weaknesses (and who hasn't a weak fourth and fifth finger?), then give him special exercises to do every day. Don't wait. Start him at once on something to strengthen his wrist action. It does not matter whether it is octaves or something of less span than an octave, but get him at it at once. If he objects, you must make it plain to him that very little development can be expected without such practice. If he is not immediately willing, he probably soon will be, when he realizes the need.

Show him the difference. Study him. Try to discover his tastes and abilities.

What would you do to improve the pupil's rhythm? What material would you use?

What would you do to strengthen the fourth and fifth fingers? What exercises?

How would you plan his practice time?

1

CHOICE OF MATERIAL

Successful teaching of music students depends, in a great measure, on a wise selection of practice material. For the piano, the choice of material is richer than for any other instrument. It can scarcely be denied, however, that there is much of a kind that may be practiced but doesn't produce results. Pupils often prefer to play such things. Select good editions, with good fingering, or else write in the fingering yourself.

Etudes which develop independence, velocity, strength of fingers and wrists, rhythmic sense, and fingering must be sought out and made use of. It is a wise plan to have several kinds of etudes going at the same time, in order to relieve monotony for the pupil: something with a distinct rhythmic problem, something for strength, and something for velocity, when the proper time comes. Sonatinas and sonatas, inventions and canons, produce better results in shorter time than the "pretty" things.

Of course, there must be the "piece" along with the others. As a reward for learning the other things, dangle something especially attractive for bait, but try to have in it some problem for development. There are ways to make all these things more interesting. (*See* PRACTICE.)

Something with running movement is better than slow pieces in which the hand has time to become heavy and be pulled down. Etudes with a range of five notes for early beginners are better for learning support, and quiet hand and finger action. Save those with a more extended range of notes until a little later. Style and expression may come later, when you consider that the pupil is ready.

Do not try to do everything at once; stay at one thing until something is accomplished. It is an excellent plan to review work occasionally. Make the pupil understand that a review is not a reflection on his progress, that he is really where he is, and then, on reviewing a piece or an etude, if he finds he can play it better than before he will be encouraged. Many students show repugnance to being "put

2

back." There really is no such thing. Talk to him a good deal: explain; tell him why; reason with him. Most students will be found reasonable.

Avoid giving practice work that is much too difficult. There are several good reasons for this. It may discourage the pupil if he cannot learn it. It may give him a wrong idea of what playing means. Pupils are often heard dragging through some fine composition at a tempo much too slow, in rhythms much too weak, and in execution in general, slovenly. Many imagine they are doing it as well as anyone could, and persevere simply because the teacher gave it to them.

Of course, there are undoubtedly occasions when giving the pupil something too hard will spur him to greater effort, and may possibly do him good, if the fingering and other requirements are carefully studied. However, make him see the difference between merely getting through something, and really playing it well.

It is hard to convince young and ambitious pupils that the main thing is how they play, and not so much what. How much better to play a simple thing really well than to ruin the more difficult piece by bad playing!

Much depends on the individual pupil, of course. Study him closely to find out his traits and ability.

Look over your teaching material carefully; annotate it; mark it for the pupil. Give him something special to do in it. He is then likely to become more interested in it. You are sure to find something suitable for every need in the enormous mass of piano literature.

Etudes that are written in pairs, that is, that present the same kind of material for the left hand that the right hand has to play, are excellent for training. Notice how many studies concern the right hand, while the left hand is used merely to peck out a banjolike accompaniment. This is scarcely the way to develop a good left-hand technique. How can we get around this? Require the left hand to play the right-hand part in the proper register, of course. Have the pupil play with both hands in unison.

Choose a composition that contains a definite problem. Don't use a Chopin ballade or a difficult nocturne when the pupil has neither technique to play it, nor sufficient ability to grasp its meaning. It is bad policy for many reasons, although it doubtless delights the pupil and his parents. It would do him much more good to study the sonatas of Mozart and Haydn for a while.

Always good foundation work first!

THE THUMB

The thumb resembles the tongue—it is difficult to tame. It is, perhaps, the most important member of the hand. By reason of its peculiar formation, it facilitates the crossing of the fingers in legato scales and arpeggios.

Untrained, the thumb is a real obstruction. If it is stiff or allowed to "cave in" at the lower joint (the one next the hand), it will be the cause of much bad playing. A certain great teacher in New York, who has written valuable books on the mastery of the piano, speaking of a certain pupil who had just come to her, said, "Oh, her thumbs are perfectly dreadful! I shall have to put her on thumb exercises alone for several months."

The thumb must be trained to slide closely from black keys down to white keys—and also to perform the reverse movement. It must be able to work over from one white key to another without any noticeable break, to do all sorts of things that may seem impossible at first. Too often thumbs are held out stiff, like a piece of wood, and thump their way over the keys. The resulting effect is very bad.

The teacher must be constantly on the watch to correct bad position and bad action in this most neglected and recalcitrant digit. It really is a finger, having three joints like the other fingers, but differently arranged. Not many pupils realize that the joint that really does the playing is down quite near the wrist joint, while in the other fingers it is the knuckle joint.

A thumb that refuses to pass under the hand with sufficient ease to play legato in arpeggios must be helped by special manipulatory exercises, performed away from the piano. But persevere and it will finally yield, though it is often slow work.

The double-jointed thumb and the unusually long thumb both must be given the most careful attention. Don't give up; single the member out and give it special exercises until it improves. The importance of a well-trained thumb can hardly be overestimated.

Try to make the thumb cling to the keys and hold its notes for the absolute full time. In legato octaves, which sometimes are necessary, the thumb has to slide forward until

5

it holds the key on the second joint, while the point reaches forward for a black key or perhaps a white key a third above or below.

Avoid "jabbing" the keys with the thumb. The thumb must be trained to hold its position when not in use, to curve around the corner of the white key, and to play independently from the joint without the help of the hand.

The thumb that pulls in under the hand at the middle joint inevitably draws the fifth finger toward it, and then we have a hand that is not adjusted to the keys. It will look more like a bird's claw than a human hand.

A thumb that is stiff and unwieldy must be given daily massages to loosen it up and make it able to pass under the hand easily enough to play legato arpeggios and scales. Such exercises, if continued every day, will in time produce good results and greatly improve the condition of the thumb. Too few teachers prescribe special thumb exercises of this sort outside of regular practice. Much can be done away from the piano; pressing the thumb under the hand, drawing it out, rolling it until the joint nearest the wrist joint is made to operate, and similar exercises. Another good one is as follows: spread the thumb out from the hand, curve the joints, hold it a little, then relax. The teacher should follow this up and make sure that the pupil forms a regular daily habit of doing it a great deal. There is absolutely no danger in such exercises, if ordinary common sense is used. Incidentally, stiff, tight fingers should be given the same treatment.

A little before Bach's time, the thumb was allowed to hang below the hand, in playing. It was thought to be too short, not the right shape, with several other disabilities. The four fingers did all the playing. No legato was attempted; perhaps it was not possible on the instruments of the day. But it is fortunate for modern keyboard players that the thumb is formed as it is, for it makes a "bridge" to carry the hand over in legato playing.

OCTAVES

Are octaves a weak spot in the musical education of many pupils? Yes and no.

No player can expect to evade them. If the hand is absolutely too small to reach them, then the case is hopeless and the player will always remain extremely limited in performance. But given a good hand, the end result goes back to preparation, or the lack of it.

Wrist exercises of some sort should be undertaken very early, even with children who cannot be expected to stretch an octave. At least, they can span a fifth or a sixth. Even with grownups it is better to begin on an interval of a sixth, until the thumb and fifth finger learn to hold a firm position, and the wrist to move loosely.

The fifth finger must be held arched so that it strikes on the end, and not flat or on the side. The thumb must learn to curve around the corner of the key, and the middle fingers must be held up and in such a position that they cannot flop on the keys. Begin by repeating an easy stretch, over and over, raising the wrist rather high, and allowing the hand to fall loosely upon the keys but never to lose position.

Listen carefully to make sure that both notes are equal in clearness. It is a very common thing to hear an octave passage in which both fingers touch the keys but only one of the fingers produces a sound.

A good octave is so difficult to acquire that its practice must be begun early and kept up continually. Learn to play them easily and without holding the body tense. Some octaves are played with the forearm, or even the arm, but in early practice, where great speed is not wanted, this is unnecessary. Only the wrist is capable of accomplishing great velocity in octaves, and indeed in many cases the wrist seems scarcely to move at all, but it does move a little.

Make a practice of playing octave studies and passages in broken octaves in both directions. Comparatively few pupils can play broken octaves, and the reason is clear— they never work at them. And that is because they are rarely asked to work at them.

Syncopated octaves and interlacing or "blind octaves" must in turn be achieved as well as legato octaves, in order to equip the player with a good octave technique.

If the hand is sufficiently large, use the fourth finger on the black keys to facilitate velocity. It is true that some teachers are against this, but there seems to be no good reason for their opposition.

Avoid playing over a great number of octave studies, or you will not be able to play any of them, as so often happens.

A good technique may be developed by using only Döring's op. 24 and staying by it until it is really learned. The variety of material is very rich; besides, any octave passage from a composition will afford good material.

For syncopated octaves, try Döring's op. 25, the last one in Kullak's *School of Octave Playing,* and the closing passage in Mendelssohn's *Rondo Capriccioso.*

For "blind" chords try William Mason's *Toccatina in A Flat.* Occasionally it will be necessary to play either the lower or the upper note in an octave louder than the other. Don't trust to luck; prepare for this by practicing it. Make the study of octaves a distinct branch of your musical education. Don't leave them to chance or luck. They won't come that way.

When a passage is to be played an octave higher, 8va . . . . is written over it. Written under a bass passage, the same direction lowers it an octave. It is called an octave line, and is simply the abbreviation for the word *ottava.* The figure 8 written under a note in the bass usually means that an octave should be played instead of a single note. The written note, of course, should be the top one.

CHORDS

Perhaps nothing in piano technique is so difficult of attainment as the ability to play chords well. One often hears chords in which the sound of the fingernails on the keys is also mixed—harsh, dry-sounding chords with an important note too weak, or an unimportant one too loud.

It is probably true that very few chords should be played so that all the notes are equally strong, as the melody usually lies in the upper voice of the chord, and ought to be made prominent. Sometimes it is necessary to bring out a line of notes in the middle, or at the bottom of a chord. A special and persistent study ought to be made of chords, but unfortunately there does not seem to be a great deal of material on the subject.

Extraneous noises—nails or fingers striking the keys so as to make a sound—should be scrupulously avoided. Practice chords with the fingertips near the keys, and use the strength in the weight of the arm.

The chord must first be spanned and the fingers brought into the shape it demands, before we play. Place the fingers close to the keys and then drop the arm suddenly, allowing the wrist joint to bend down. It rises at once to position, after playing.

Always see that the wrist is flexible. Allow it to move downward a little on striking a chord, and you will, in time, be able to get rid of the dry, hard-sounding chord.

Play the chord and bring up all the fingers very quickly, except the top note, then all except the lower note, and so on with each of the notes. This leads to the ability to bring out any single note desired. Study the notes slowly and listen to them carefully.

Saint-Saëns has written a few good studies along this line. There is also a good one in Moscheles' op. 70 that should be studied in every conceivable way—held, staccato, holding the top note, then the bottom note, playing arpeggio in both directions, forte, and again piano—repeating each chord, and again repeating the chord as a quick grace note.

Other chord exercises will be found in Czerny's op. 337,

Forty Daily Studies, and in the Pischna, Tausig, and Jonas piano schools. A pupil must not be given the impression that his teacher is simply trying to keep him busy by having him try all these various ways of practice. He must understand that in order to fully develop his touch he needs to practice a great many different ways. Have him take chord CEGC, hold it while you count two, then, on count three, spring to the same notes an octave higher, making it sound as connected as possible, leaving the last one short. Have him follow up the scale in the same manner.

At first, it seems rather futile to try to play out the top or melody note full and keep all the rest piano, but it must and can be learned, with perseverance.

The last seven numbers in Czerny's op. 802, book II, offer excellent chord practice, and Moscheles' op. 70, no. 2, is excellent.

Ultramodern composers write chords that sometimes sound impossible if all the notes are played equally loud, but by playing the dissonant notes softer than the others the effect is at once changed into a strange new color, and affects the ear in a different way.

Arpeggios or rolled chords should be held down (if possible) the full length of the chord. For special effects this may vary. If the chords in both hands are to be rolled from the lowest bass note, a long undulating line covers both chords. If the lowest notes in both hands are to be played simultaneously, two separate lines are marked. In old editions, a vertical slur line may be found. Its meaning is the same.

1.   2.

1.   Begin the lowest notes in both hands simultaneously.
2.   Begin the lowest note in the left hand.

RHYTHM

What is rhythm exactly? Here it would be easy to get into a lengthy discussion, the subject of rhythm being complicated and extensive, but to be concise, let us say that, in music, rhythm is the element that marks the tempo of the composition, the recurring of the accent at regular intervals, as *one*, two, three, or *one*, two, *one*, two, with a natural stress on the one. In Greek, from which it is derived, the word means "to flow." It is "the flow" that gives life to music (and most other things, for that matter), and it is more than melody or harmony. It is the most important element in music. Try recalling some theme by its rhythm without the musical tones and you will find it comparatively easy, in most cases, while if a well-known melody is played in another rhythm it may sound unfamiliar. Rhythm must always be present, although some compositions demand a stronger rhythm than others.

In some compositions, the rhythm is so complex as to be confusing. Music without rhythm is monotonous, and in rare cases it is intended to be so. Note Palmgren's *Isle of Shadows*. A hazy, misty effect, without much life, is what the music calls for.

An arbitrary accent, or sforzando, may upset and absorb for a time the natural rhythm, as in the last few measures of the first movement of Beethoven's op. 2, no. 1.

Cultivate rhythm in your pupils with great perseverance. If you discover a natural weakness among any of them, then your efforts must be doubled. Use all sorts of rhythmic changes on etudes, scales, and passages. Furthermore, try to get the pupil to think the rhythm as he is playing it. Have him write it down on paper. It is astonishing how many pupils who otherwise play pretty well fail in this. It shows that there is a weakness both in drill and in instruction, but they are weaknesses that can easily be remedied. Try to accent *one* certain note in playing a scale or an exercise, without accenting the one next to it, as so frequently happens. Overaccentuate in practicing to make it impressive to the sense. Make use of agogic accents, or held accents, for the same purpose. Try in every way to get pupils to think rhythmically. It is uphill work in many cases, but by constant drill a sense of rhythm may be developed; without drill little can be expected.

Meter is frequently confused with rhythm and given the same definition, even by authorities. It seems certain, however, that it embraces more. Rhythm has to do with accentuation, while meter is more a grouping of phrases and measures, bearing some analogy to meter in verse. Illustrate on the piano with the first part of Chopin's *Ballade in F Major* to show meter.

Hymn tunes also illustrate meter—eights and sevens, common meter, and others.

THE TOUCHES

The pianist who expects to succeed with only one touch can be compared to a person driving an automobile in which only one cylinder of the engine is operating. He will not get very far. One nevertheless observes many players who seem to have no ambition beyond getting the right notes and playing loudly. Variety by means of various touches or various phrasings seems to have no place in their work.

Every pianist who hopes to be interesting must equip himself with a good crisp finger staccato touch for light, rapid passages, when a wrist staccato is not possible. He also must have a good close or overlapping legato for melody passages, and for variety the slurred staccato, or negative staccato, as Scharwenka called it, or more commonly, portamento. The effect is the same, whatever it be called. Some contend that the term "portamento" is correctly applied to vocal effects only. Let us see if this can be true.

The same effect—a sliding down on one continuous tone —is used on the violin and other bowed string instruments. What does the word mean, literally? Simply, "carrying." There is more than one way to carry: up, down, over, across, or under. Certainly its meaning should not be restricted to vocal effects, or to any one instrument. Most pupils see the dots, but neglect to notice the slur above, and thus play exactly as if the notes were marked half staccato.

All great teachers who have laid down rules for the length of notes under the different markings agree that a note with a dot and a slur is to be given three quarters of its original length, really carrying (portamento) it over a little.

One must admit that this touch, when it is transferred to the piano, loses considerable of its original effect. On the clavichord, for which it is supposed to have been invented, its effect was much more distinctive owing to the ability, by a light afterpressure of the key, to produce something akin to a slight swell accompanied by a negligible sharpening of pitch. All this has gone with the passing of the old instruments; however, the cultivation of the portamento touch is well worth the time and pains that may be given it by the student. It is practicable only in moderate tempo, as beyond a certain speed all the different touches merge into a leggiero or crisp legato.

Do not fail to urge pupils to cultivate all the shades of touch; and one must keep repeating that a good time to do this is while studying etudes, which become many times more interesting and valuable if varied in touch, rhythm, and phrasing, from day to day.

Karl Klindworth, the great Berlin piano teacher, was once asked by someone in class what he considered to be the foundation, or ground touch. He thought a moment, then said that a very crisp legato, almost leggiero, such as one uses in playing Czerny etudes, defined it. Have pupils build their other touches on this.

THE HOLD

The hold (*fermata,* in Italian; *Pause,* in German; *point d'arrêt,* in French) is printed thus: ⌒. Usually it should be approached by a ritardando and the note under the sign should be prolonged. There is no fixed rule about how long it should be held, but it should give the effect of a stop, and if the note is a long note it is usually considered that half again the length of the note is enough. Sometimes the word "lunga" is found, which means, of course, a long stop. If the note in question is a short note, such as an eighth or a sixteenth, it is often prolonged several times its original length. It is a matter of musical taste and instinct, but it must be good taste, of course. Busoni said that a hold should be a place of rest for the listener as well as the performer.

It usually makes the music more eloquent if a moment of silence occurs after the hold, before picking up the tempo. This has come to be applied in piano music less from necessity, as in the case of singers and wind-instrument players who, when they have made a ritardando followed by a hold, must have a moment in which to recover their breath before continuing, than because it is the natural thing to do in music. Occasionally, if so marked, one approaches the fermata in time, and goes on without pause.

THE RITARDANDO

Many words used in music have something of the meaning of ritardando in them: for instance, the French word "cedez," frequently used in French editions of music, which means literally to give way; the word "suivez," which means to follow the solo in a probable ritardando; the German term "langsamer werdend"; the Italian words "calando," to let down; "slargando," "allargando," growing broader; "rallentando," slowing; and several others.

Brahms constantly uses the word "sostenuto" in the same sense. Always keep in mind that the endings "ando," "endo," and "ente" are the same thing as "ing" in English and mean that the action is continued to the end. A good ritardando begins in time and grows evenly slower to the point when "a tempo" (in time) is written.

The endings "uto" and "ato" mean exactly the same as "ed" in English: that the action is completed. A ritenuto is a retarded passage instead of one gradually growing slower. Unfortunately, many composers abuse this term and write simply the abbreviation "rit.," so that the player is left to guess at what is meant.

Care must be taken not to make a great deal of ritardando when the words "poco (a little) ritardando" occur. On the other hand, molto (very much) ritardando is often mistakenly passed over with a slight relaxation of the time. Fine performers sometimes do not understand the meaning of these words and a great many others—certainly a deplorably weak spot in their education.

The term "pochetto" (very little), made up of the word "poco" and a diminutive ending, and the word "pochettino" (very, very little), containing two diminutive endings, should, of course, be observed as indicated.

At the close of Brahms' *Rhapsody in G Minor,* he has written a natural ritardando that is indicated by the length of the notes, and, of course, he expected it to be sufficient. The same effect is found in Dvořák's *On the Holy Mount,* and Liszt's *Gondoliera.* It would be unwise to add any marks to such compositions.

Always gauge the ritardando by the length of time there is in which to make it. If it covers several measures, there is time to be quite gradual about it; if it is shorter, then it necessitates a sudden holding back. It sometimes happens that a composer writes the word several times, at intervals, in a rather extended passage, by which he means that it is to be extremely gradual until the end of the passage is reached. Or he may mean to take up the tempo after each ritardando. Remember, the slowest point is just before the tempo starts again.

The words "morendo," dying, and "smorzando," fading away, may combine a diminishing of tone with a ritardando. Pupils should beware of continually making ritardandos when none are intended, as they may be exaggerating, which is always bad style.

Remember, the word "enough" is a golden word in art. Too much is often ludicrous and absolutely defeats the end. The words "ritardando" and "rallentando" do not normally imply a diminishing of tone, simply a slowing of time. In a composition containing a repeat, even though marked ritardando, it is better taste not to hold back too much at the end of the section, the first time through. Save the broader ritardando for the last time. The reason is obvious. Ordinarily, the end of a piece may be broadened in order to give a sense of finality. In certain pieces of brilliant and snappy nature this would be entirely out of place. They must end with a dash, in order to be effective.

Schumann sometimes wrote ritardando several times without indicating a tempo. What does he mean? Simply that one is to pick up tempo between times. You cannot go on "ritarding" forever.

Don't play a passage ritardando without reason. It is likely to become tiresome.

THE PEDAL

Anton Rubinstein once said: "The pedal is the soul of the piano," and nothing is more true than that its proper use can make good playing better. Wrongly used, however, it can ruin the piece being played. The pupil must be trained to listen carefully and learn to distinguish a blurred sound so he can avoid making it. Let him try this. Sound C and D together with the pedal down, then hold either one with the finger and release the pedal. If his ear does not distinguish the change, he must keep trying until it does.

Make use of simple pedal exercises in every lesson until he begins to use the pedal intelligently. Naturally, the pedal goes down after the new note is played and must be released at the exact moment of playing the next tone so that the pedal syncopates, so to speak.

One has to test the pedal on every piano, as some seem to produce a blur more easily than others, with the same effort. Pedaling that sounds well in a small room will often be found entirely inadequate for a larger hall, where space swallows up the vibrations. Therefore pedal to suit the occasion. Listen well to your pedal effects.

One must not be misled by the marks in some compositions, notably Beethoven's so-called *Moonlight Sonata*. He marked the first movement "senza sordini," which means to raise the dampers by putting down the damper pedal, and there is no indication farther along that it is to be changed. It is conceivable that Beethoven played whole pages without changing the pedal on the piano of his day; but to do this on the modern piano would produce an exceedingly bad effect, because today the pedal controls a much greater sonority than it did in Beethoven's lifetime. In playing Bach, Scarlatti, and, in fact, all the old classic composers, it must not be forgotten that there was no pedal in those days and that in composing they did not have to consider it.

Too much pedal may ruin the delicate tissue of compositions by these older masters; not that it should be left out entirely, but it should be used carefully. Avoid noises of the foot on the pedal. The sole of the shoe should be kept close against the pedal, and care should be taken not to allow the dampers to thump back on the strings too suddenly, which also makes a disturbing noise. Pedal noises may ruin the effect of playing. Pianos differ in respect to pedal noises, and this, too, must be taken into consideration.

A very great pianist of our own day is remembered by many because in climaxes he pounded the pedal (and even the floor) so loudly with his left foot that the noise resounded through the hall. No doubt he was utterly unconscious of doing it.

In a composition like Palmgren's *Isle of Shadows,* which is impressionistic, and in which the atmosphere of weird forms emerging from misty shadows is the principal effect desired, a great deal of pedal should be used. Needless to say, the piano should be in exquisite tune or the effect will be more than atmospheric.

Some compositions, when exceeding lightness of effect is desired, are better played with almost no pedal. Be careful that the pedal is not used monotonously. Don't let pupils pedal every composition the same way. Have them study its effects carefully.

The middle, or sostenuto, pedal on the grand piano certainly deserves wider use. Many players never touch it. Magnificent effects are made possible by its proper use. For sustaining low bass notes through successive harmonies or for holding tones in the middle register of the piano it is very valuable; and it may be used to produce otherwise unobtainable effects.

One effect is the "half release," produced by putting the pedal only part way down and changing very quickly on the new harmony, so as to catch and hold the low tone. (*See* Arthur Whiting's *Pedal Studies.*)

Another is the "echo pedal" effect, obtained by striking a certain chord very strongly with the pedal down, then, while holding the pedal, putting down the keys of another chord silently, without striking them, and releasing the pedal suddenly. You will find you have the new chord under your fingers, but with the effect of an echo. This effect is used in Schumann's *Carnaval,* op. 9, and seems very mysterious when heard for the first time.

The una corda pedal makes the tone softer and also

changes its quality. In the older pianos, which had two wires tuned in unison, this pedal pushed the hammers to the right so that they struck only one of the strings, hence the term "una corda," one string; and "due corde" meant the release of this pedal to allow two strings to sound. Modern pianos have three wires to most of the tones and the hammers literally strike two of them when the una corda pedal is used, but the term "una corda" is still used to indicate the effect. This is now an inaccuracy that ought to be changed to "due corde" for pedal and "tre corde" for release, instead of "una corda" for pedal and "tre corde" for release. Of course, it won't be. These things stay.

Don't abuse this pedal. Learn to play pianissimo without it, but, of course, use it at times. It is a good idea to change the quality of tone sometimes. Many players and teachers seem to suffer from superstitition regarding the una corda pedal. They think it better not to use it at all. This is hard to understand. What is it for, this pedal? It relieves monotony in tune color. Use it, therefore.

TEMPO RUBATO

The words "tempo rubato" mean robbed time, in the sense of prolonging certain notes and making others a little shorter. The result should be an easy give-and-take style. It is attributed to Chopin, but it surely must have been known and used before his time.

Chopin, however, seems to have been the first to extensively exploit this style, and for years it was frequently referred to as the "Chopin tempo." The "Chopin rubato" has been declared to be so absolutely intangible that no words can describe it. This seems a little absurd, though it is true that there is no clear way to indicate it exactly in words. Surely, the plunging, jerking wiggle that one frequently hears as "rubato" is far from what Chopin intended or practiced.

To play Chopin's music in a perfectly stiff and angular style is certain to remove much of the beauty, but this is true of other music, too, and is not confined to Chopin's music alone. Read Constantin Sternberg's essay entitled *Tempo Rubato* and remember that to carry any form of expression exactly far enough is the test of artistry. Exaggerations are apt to cheapen the effect.

There are, of course, many times where no rubato can be permitted, such as a march (*marcia*) where rhythm is most important. If a march is played unsteadily, it suggests dizziness, or something worse! Don't be afraid to play exactly in time. Some pupils seem to have the idea that in order to play artistically one must always be putting in ritardandos or jump over some other passage as if the player had to finish quickly to catch a train.

There is no great mystery about rubato. It can be described; and when not exaggerated it is highly effective—in the right place.

Ask pupils to play some examples in class.

DAILY SETTING-UP EXERCISES

One will hear it said sometimes that there is no such thing as a "daily" exercise. Perhaps there is no such thing as "daily" bread, if one wishes to look at it that way. Many may shrink from the idea of practicing the same exercise every day throughout a lifetime—and no wonder! However, that is not what is meant in speaking of the class of exercises called "daily" exercises. Far from it.

It is hardly possible that any pianist will deny the necessity of a "limbering up" or "get going" sort of exercise before starting out on the more intricate things. The finger and arm muscles relax at night; and things, so to speak, get out of the fingers and must be brought back into shape constantly.

In the literature of exercises for the piano we have perhaps a richer assortment than for any other instrument. Therefore one need not stick to any single set. However, I think that each individual, after years of experience, will be inclined to single out a few favorite exercises that he has found do him some especial good and bring the quickest results. The weak fourth and fifth fingers, so difficult to equalize with the others, need special exercises from the very beginning, if one is determined to train them well.

You will want to work them sometimes for strength, sometimes for velocity, and constantly for lightness. It seems that one can never acquire absolute sureness in playing some passages in difficult skips, and there is nothing to do but to keep at them daily. It also seems impossible to keep certain polyphonic figures in the fingers except by constant rehearsing. Bach's gay and lilting fugue in B flat major will be found to contain a number of such spots.

Always have some technical problem that you are trying to solve, and be sure you conquer it. Experiment with technique. Play passages in octaves that are written in single notes, or with both hands, the left hand playing the same notes in the lower range. It is a curious fact that in all collections of etudes there occur very few good ones for the left hand as compared with the number for the right hand. Get around this by learning the right-hand part with the left hand and working out a good fingering suited to the left hand.

Try frequently to transpose exercises into another key. Change the fingering. Change the rhythms, accents, dynamics; in short, try in every way to make the exercise more difficult than it is in its original form. There really is no other way to practice with benefit. Always try to keep the mind busy while practicing technics. Students who look out the window, carry on a conversation, or eat something while pretending to work might just as well be doing something else. They will make very little progress. Practice continually the scales in several forms: staccato, legato, accented in various ways, canonic, thirds, contrary movement, and similar movements. Arpeggios are of first importance. Among the most valuable of these is the set by William Mason, published by Presser under the title of *Touch and Technic*. Those of Pischna, Tausig, and Czerny, especially op. 337, are all excellent.

Don't forget that it is the *way* we work that does the good, rather than the exercises themselves, and that day by day we are forming habits, good or bad, that are going to stay with us. Try to make them good habits.

The following exercises, studies, and textbooks will be found helpful in planning a course of daily setting-up exercises.

Brahms: *Technical Studies,* published by N. Simrock.
Czerny: Op. 337; *Forty Daily Studies in All Styles,* published by Peters.
Czerny: Op. 802, Books I and II; *Chords, Independence, Scales, Etc.,* published by Lemoine.
Doring: Op. 38, Book II; *Exercises for Passing the Thumb.*
Floridia: *Piano Exercises for Finger Stretching, Etc.,* published by C. Fisher.
Frey: *Exercises for Passing the Thumb,* published by Steingraber.
Jonas: *Complete Piano School.* Extensive work.
Joseffy: *Complete Piano School.* Extensive work.
Landon, Charles W.: *Playing Two Notes against Three,* published by Presser.
Levy, H.: *The Chopin Technique.*

MacDowell: *Technical Studies,* published by Boosey and Hawkes.

Mantey: *Unequal Rhythms* (No. 2750), published by Litolf.

Mason, William: *Pianoforte Technics.*

Mason, William: *Touch and Technic.*

Moszkowski: Op. 64, Books I, II and III; *School of Scales and Double Notes.*

Philipp: *Exercises in Holds,* published by Durand. Exactly the thing most players need.

Philipp: *Preparatory Exercises,* published by Durand.

Philipp: *The Trill in Beethoven,* published by Oliver Ditson.

Pischna: *Complete Piano Studies,* published by Schirmer.

Plaidy: *Complete Piano Studies.*

Schneider: Op. 11; *Stretching Exercises,* published by Boosey and Hawkes.

Schytte: Op. 75; in ten parts of six studies each, broken chords, shake, tremolo, octaves, alternation of hands, rhythms, polyrhythms, legato, staccato, and left hand.

Schytte: *Forty Pedal Studies: Chords, Thirds, and Sixths.*

Smith, W. G.: *Five Minute Studies for Fourth and Fifth Fingers,* published by Church.

Sternberg: *Studies in Repetition Technique,* published by Schirmer.

Sternberg: Op. 118; *First Studies in Polyrhythms,* published by Schirmer.

Tausig: *Daily Studies.* Difficult irregular passages.

Wiehmayer: *Scale School and Arpeggio School,* published by Boosey and Hawkes. Thumb exercises.

Wiehmayer: *Daily Studies.*

KEEPING TIME

Pupils who can't count, who won't count, who are too proud to count, who think they can evade counting by doing it some other way, who count, but in a rambling, uneven manner —all these call for patience. Such players are apt to be a nuisance. Pupils must count straight and play up to the count, and not the reverse.

Make them understand from the first that it is impossible to become a good musician without this ability, and that it is no disgrace to count, but a sign of superior intelligence. Insist on it from the beginning.

Those who object to counting aloud soon forget all about it, and cease to count at all. It is a help to hear the count, though it doesn't need to be kept up after one can really keep good time.

Most of this can be done during the technical exercises— Plaidy, or whatever series is being used—and will be unnecessary in other things. Teach the pupil how to count out the difficult places on the short notes so he will know when he is right. Afterward, the words need not be said aloud, but the mind must still formulate the count. And don't slight the rests!

Begin early to cultivate a sense of metronome marks. There are many people leading choirs and beating time for small orchestras and glee clubs who have not the slightest idea of what is meant by M.M. (Maelzel's Metronome). Or what ♩=100 means! Or ♩.=♩ or ♩.=♩ at the beginning of a *new* movement. There seems to be no excuse for such ignorance. So many beats in a minute of time, ♩=84.

On being asked what M.M. stands for, pupils have been known to give such guesses as "metronome mark," and even "my metronome."

Tell them how the metronome came to be invented. Many musicians say they never pay any attention to metronome marks. But they are making a mistake, and probably spoiling the music. The marks may in some cases be wrong, but in general they give a good idea of the tempo.

NERVOUSNESS IN PLAYING

A number of things, or combinations of them, may cause nervousness in a player. Some of them are the realization of insufficient preparation, poor health, overwork and consequent exhaustion, wrong mental attitude, and inexperience in appearing before the public.

Nervousness usually shows itself at one of three different times, and sometimes it lasts through all of them: before starting to play; while playing; and after playing, which is the least serious.

Nervousness and fear are different things. There are few artists who are not nervous to some degree before a performance. Nervousness actually seems to key some of them up and makes them do their best. But real artists are seldom frightened.

Here are some remedies for nervousness.

Be absolutely sure you know what you are going to play and that you have allowed it to season and settle a considerable length of time.

Be able to think it clear through—pedaling, dynamics, and tempo—and be sure you have rehearsed on the piano and in the room where you are going to play. Try to be quiet and in full control of your senses just before going out on the stage.

Often the chatter of some well-meaning friends may make it difficult for you. Try to remember that your performance is not your last chance, and that even if you should forget you will not be in disgrace. Be deliberate in beginning to play; wait until you have established the correct tempo in your mind. Many players are upset and thrown off balance at the very beginning because they start too fast.

Often it is a help to close the eyes for a moment, and to fill the lungs deeply. Try to play for yourself, and shut out the idea of the audience. Lose yourself in the music, if possible.

Nervousness can be overcome in time, and the best way to help banish it is frequent practice in playing before people.

Try to induce a few friends to listen to you play—that is always a help.

When you habitually practice in the same room and on the same piano, you unconsciously memorize the way everything looks, and you feel at ease in your surroundings. A complete change of scene is very apt to divert your attention. Naturally, you must overcome this tendency toward distraction by rehearsing in different places as much as possible. Scarcely any player goes through a concert without some slight mistake, so don't take it too seriously should you make one. Make up your mind to do your very best—then do it.

PHRASING AND INFLECTION

Phrasing in music means the grouping together of notes to punctuate the music and increase its significance. It might be called music punctuation. In some ways it has a close analogy to the grouping of words in language to clarify the meaning. Phrases may consist of two notes or any number of notes, and they are usually covered by a slur. Generally speaking, the end of the line indicates that a break is to be made, although there are times in rapid movements when this seems impracticable because it gives a lame effect, which is bad. Another way to accomplish it is by means of accents, either dynamic or agogic. A slight holding of the first note of the intended phrase will produce the effect of marking it without breaking it, in rapidly moving passages; or it may be that accenting will answer the same purpose. A long phrase may be subdivided into smaller phrases, which need not interfere with the phrase's meaning.

Some of the older composers left phrasing entirely to the taste of the player, and this absence of markings accounts for the variety of phrase indications in Bach, for example. They have been supplied by editors, and in no two editions are they exactly alike. Some are better than others, and some are downright bad. Choose the best, but be sure to observe some phrasing. Language is stupid without pauses and inflections; music is also.

There are many nameless little touches, stresses, prolongations of tones, and other embellishments that are heard in the playing of a great artist, that, in years of playing, might never occur to the student who does not listen carefully. The best way to acquire them is from a good teacher or by carefully observing the playing of fine artists. Be careful not to accent notes of less importance in the measure, or group, such as the anacrusis. Make it sound of less importance than the ictus. In successive phrases of two notes, be careful to soften down on the second or last note. A phrase well inflected naturally diminishes at the end.

FINGERING

Pupils constantly ask what is the best way to finger a passage. There is really no law to compel one to finger a passage in a certain way, although there is a certain logic in fingering that ought to be observed. If you have selected a good edition, well fingered, give the fingering a fair trial; practice it hard; and if in the end you decide it won't do, then try another fingering. It is said that Liszt used to practice a certain fingering several weeks before deciding to adopt it. For you, another fingering, or even a slight change of fingering, may cause the difficulties to vanish. Don't shun a certain fingering because at first sight it may appear to be odd or unnatural or too difficult. Give it a good trial. Too often, what seems awkward and unmanageable at first, proves in the end to be absolutely reliable, when thoroughly learned.

Practice the same passage with various fingerings, but only after one is thoroughly learned. Some may fear that this leads to confusion, and it may seem that way at first—but persevere. If, by chance, the fingering previously learned should slip, the tendency is to save oneself with one of the other fingerings, so the result is far from disastrous. If your pupils, after practicing a certain fingering thoroughly, cannot master it, give them another for a while, and on returning to the first it then will often prove to be easy.

Pay a great deal of attention to fingering. It is the only way to be sure of the notes and to insure a good performance. Fingering builds technique. If one learns a standard fingering for a conventional musical figure, it usually remains good wherever the same figure occurs.

EMBELLISHMENTS

Trills, mordents, turns, and appoggiaturas of both kinds all come under the head of embellishments, or graces, in music, and must be executed very neatly and clearly and, as a rule, with a little less tone than the main melody line receives. They are difficult to do, and must receive special study for their successful execution. In beginning to play trills, it is always better to give a pupil an exact number of notes to play until he can play those clearly and evenly, and it helps greatly to accent them regularly. Often a trill will come out at the end, and seem to fill in the space better when played in triplets, allowing the last two notes of the triplet to represent the two small notes printed in the trill.

A trill is apt to sound bad if finished badly, while a rather poor trill nicely finished sometimes succeeds in deceiving the ear. Pupils are often misled by seeing an acciaccatura placed before the note to be trilled, and try to play it first, and then trill. Remember, the mark only means that the trill begins on that note.

In the eighteenth century, trills usually began on the upper auxiliary note and ended without the customary turn of today. In Bach's music, in a trill on a dotted note, it is the custom to stop trilling on the dot.

Artists are likely to trill with three fingers instead of two on trills of long duration, thus the trill on CD would be fingered 1-3-2-3-1-3-2-3, and so on. This rests the hand and produces more clearness. The same fingering holds good on mordents: 1-3-2 or 3-1-2. It is not easy to acquire a beautiful, even trill; the technique must be constantly studied in a most persistent manner.

Often a note marked to be trilled is of such short duration that nothing more than a triplet is expected. See Haydn's *Sonata in D Major*. There are even places in Mozart's music where a trill is marked over a rapid sixteenth note, which cannot possibly be executed as a trill. A rapid grace note is all that can be expected.

All ornamental figures like turns, mordents, and trills must be executed without clumsiness. It often happens that they turn out to be anything but ornamental if played heavily or clumsily. Do not leave them to chance; study them in all keys and with various fingerings. The mordent is taken from the Italian word "mordante," and is explained by our own word "mordant" (biting), which is derived from the French word "mordre" (to bite). It literally bites its way out of the beginning of the note's value. The mordent with a downward stroke through it is commonly accepted as the real mordent: ♣. It is played with rapid alternation from the written note to the one a half step lower. The upward mordent ∿ is called inverted, and uses the note above the written one. Try to finger the notes with a change of fingers and you will learn to bring them out clearly and without effort.

The early composers used a multiplicity of signs and combinations of signs that are now largely obsolete. Even in those times they sometimes disagreed with each other about the way they were to be executed. Turns used to be played by the way the sign stood: ∾ beginning on the note above, ∾ beginning on the note below. Most of these signs are disregarded by composers today. They use one sign for ∿ but it is usually safe to assume that if the note following the note on which the turn is written is above it, the turn may begin on the note above the written note:

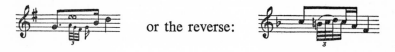

or the reverse:

This, however, is not always true when a turn is arbitrarily written out, as in *Götterdämmerung*:

A turn is to be considered as a sort of connecting loop and should be executed, as has been said, with a little lighter tone, to be graceful. Most good editions of music explain turns in footnotes.

Grace notes, or appoggiaturas, are of two kinds, long and short. Today, the short one is usually written by a small eighth with a stroke through it; but in former times any note of short duration, such as a sixteenth or a thirty-second, was employed, and the stroke was meant to

scratch away its natural time value and make it extremely short. It is perhaps better to call it an acciaccatura, or something crushed, as it is literally crushed against the following note. The word "appoggiare" in Italian means literally to support. In this sense the note is better understood by playing it than listening to it. It seems to support itself on the following note. Composers rarely write grace notes today but as we constantly have to deal with music written long ago, we must understand them.* They usually get just about the amount of time they would get if they were large notes and the note following them would have to yield to them. Thus:

19.

---

* A very useful little book, *Ornaments and Embellishments in Music,* by Clarence G. Hamilton, is published by Oliver Ditson Co.

TERMINOLOGY

Urge your pupils to study the meanings of the words found in music. Most of them are Italian, because in the cinquecento and later, music was reborn in Italy, or took a fresh start, and in all countries where music is practiced today the Italian terms are still used. They have become part of the universal music language.

It is appalling how many students haven't the slightest idea of the meaning of even the most common of these words. Many students do not even notice that they are there, or attach but slight importance to them, while others, in ignorance of their meaning, often do exactly the opposite of what is indicated. This ignorance is not entirely confined to students, unfortunately.

The proper pronunciation should also be taught the student. Such mispronunciations as stringendo with a hard "g," dolce as a one-syllable word, and a multitude of others, are too frequently heard. If one will only take a little trouble, there is always a way to learn the correct pronunciation, and it may prevent future embarrassment.

PLAYING A MELODY AND THE
ACCOMPANIMENT

A melody is a "song" on the piano. In playing, it should be highlighted, in contrast to the parts that are not as important. A melody must rise and fall, for if it is perfectly flat—the notes all having the same dynamic value—it is bound to be stupid and uninteresting. By thumping, pounding, or hammering out a melody above a loud accompaniment, many pupils imagine that they are "bringing out" the melody, or playing "big." They are certainly doing both, but they are not playing melodiously or intelligently. It is said that Liszt always listened to the great singers of his day, especially the tenor Rubini, who was a supreme artist, and tried to make the piano sound the same way. All the little sobs and sighs and holds and sudden drops, from forte to piano, he employed to make the piano as vocal as possible. Naturally, a very close and overlapping legato touch is necessary for this. The pedal may help, but it cannot take the place of touch.

The most natural thing to do is to crescendo in an ascending passage and diminish coming down. This is not always strictly to be observed, however. Sometimes the reverse is more effective.

If the same passage recurs a number of times, try not to play it just the same way every time. It becomes monotonous and shows a lack of originality.

Don't be afraid to experiment with a melodic passage; try it over and over again, alone, and decide where the climax should be, which note you want to bring out especially. This you may do by giving it a dynamic accent, that is, giving it more tone, or by an agogic accent, that is, giving it a little more time, or, frequently, both. After the climax, drop down a little in tone, then try it with the accompaniment. In short, study it intensively. If you do this you will find that your melodies lose their angular stiffness and begin to sing more like a voice. Try it with some of Chopin's nocturnes, the one in D flat, with Schubert, or with Liszt's "Du Bist die Ruh."

Now we must carefully consider the accompaniment,

which must never be conspicuous or get too far into the fore-ground.

The best kind of accompanist for a soloist is the one who follows every turn of the solo from rubato to con brio, who brings out everything he should, who reflects every change of mood in the text of song—if it be a song—and yet who never tries to "run away with the show," to use a common expression. Many great soloists fail absolutely as ensemble players or as accompanists because they cannot subordinate themselves.

Anything in an accompaniment in a nocturne or romanza that calls particular attention to the accompaniment as a whole is to be avoided. This does not preclude the bringing out of a single note or a succession of notes now and then, when they form an interesting little melody. An effect like accenting strongly a single note in order to prolong it through a series of changing harmonies in the other parts is good but it should not be exaggerated. Always play on the notes form-ing a progression thus:

Avoid drumming on a repeated note to make a monotonous effect. See Chopin's *Prelude in D Flat,* which has so many A flats in the left hand. Try to play them so they will not in-trude on the consciousness of the listener.

The left-hand part in Chopin's *Nocturne in D Flat* is a fine example. We have often heard this begun and played throughout in a jerky, rickety fashion, imagined by the player to be rubato, but if the listener gives full attention to the bass rather than the melody, he will hear how queer it is. Naturally this is a great blemish.

The melody often stays on a long note, lasting one or two measures, which gives it no chance to be interesting; then the accompaniment may come forward and be very inter-esting indeed. Sometimes the positions of melody and accompaniment are reversed—melody in the left hand and accompaniment in the right—but the same relation between the two should be preserved.

Sometimes two melodies of equal importance occur, one in either hand; in that case, play them accordingly.

In a general way the accompaniment should follow the shading and effects in the right hand, but always considerably softer. The dynamic marks generally indicate this, but very few pupils look at them.

In ensemble music be quick to observe where there is a purely accompanimental passage, and don't play it too loud. This fault might well be called the besetting sin of pianists. The string players are left to struggle against being drowned out, while the pianist holds their heads under water.

Good ensemble music consists of a distribution of solo passages between all players. When you come to such a passage, of course, play it as yours, but always with respect to the other players.

The test of musicianship is "doing things to the music," not queer things, of course, but legitimate things. It isn't difficult to play the notes, but that, after all, is only the first step. Someone has said very wisely, "Oh, yes! Play as you feel, but you must feel right about music." As you think and feel about things, so you really are: right or wrong.

SIGHT READING

Sight reading is sometimes a natural gift, but more often than not it has to be acquired. A musician who cannot read at sight readily has only a slim chance of success. A number of obstacles stand in the way of reading readily at sight. Among the outstanding ones is, first, the inability to decipher and sense the rhythmic figures at a glance—to be able to play easily exactly twice as fast or three times as fast as you have been playing certain notes.

Lack of familiarity with the keyboard is another. Here, practicing scales and arpeggios daily can help. The right finger is thus trained to seek automatically the right note in reading. Also, by practicing all kinds of difficult figures and rhythmic patterns, one becomes entirely familiar with them and is able to play them quickly. Nothing improves one's sight-reading ability so much as reading a good deal, either alone or with someone who is a good reader, perhaps another pianist or singer or violinist. There is something stimulating about playing duets that brings out one's best. Besides, it is one of the best possible ways to enrich one's acquaintance with music in general—the great symphonies and overtures, and other forms.

Let us note several things that may help. At the start, don't be too particular to play all the notes. Keep going, and don't lose the count and stop. It is easy to pick up and go on if the count is still in mind, but if you lose it and have to stop there is nothing to do but to begin again.

Don't try to read every single note. Read all arpeggios or broken or varied chords simply as chords—and who does not read a chord more by the shape of it, or as a group of notes, than by the separate notes? You are playing in D major, say. Runs in this key will most naturally fall into the fingering of the D major scale, which, of course, you must know. Arpeggios, Alberti basses, and such will scarcely have to be deciphered.

At first, don't try to read too fast, but try to look a little ahead so you will not be surprised by what is coming. In reading with someone else, never try to go back and correct a mistake—you are sure to be left behind. It would scarcely seem necessary to mention anything obvious, yet it occurs frequently in the case of readers. Skip a few notes, make a leap and catch up—but do not stop if you can help it.

Before beginning to play, look carefully at the sharps or flats at the beginning of the piece (the key signature) and try to sense the key. Look carefully at the time signature and get the rhythm established in the mind. Look at the tempo mark, and naturally one must know the meaning of all the terms occurring in music in order not to be misled. Many players ignore them, hence their tempo is far from right. Try to get in mind at once the character of the composition, whether it is solemn, playful, or graceful; whether it is sonorous, light and dry, or grotesque. You cannot take in all these things while you are still a beginner, but a quick grasp of them must be your ultimate aim, if you expect to give the correct interpretation to a composition.

Read all sorts of things: accompaniments to songs, sonatas, transcriptions, and the like, but don't stop to perfect them. Do that later.

Start with the firm determination to learn to read readily and accurately, observing all the dynamic and expression marks, and don't forget that this ability is one of the musician's greatest assets.*

---

* An excellent book on sight reading is *Playing at Sight,* by R. T. White, published by Curwen and Sons, London.

RELAXATION

No one doubts the usefulness of relaxation. One must seek it and practice it continually, for many reasons. It saves wear on the nerves; it makes playing sound more spontaneous. One can play longer without getting tired. Just the same, beware of confusing proper relaxation with the limp, flabby, spineless condition that many pupils get into in their efforts to achieve relaxation.

Many teachers keep calling on their pupils to loosen up, but they never mention point, clarity, and precision of touch. One cannot pick up any object without tensing the muscles somewhat, but when the object is put down again there is no need to hold the muscles in the same tensed condition. Muscles were made to be flexed and then relaxed. Remember that in order to get much of a tone, the finger points must always have a firm feeling; and that it is always easier to play in a relaxed way after the muscles have become strong than in the beginning when they are weak and one is often obliged, in holding a hand position, to use a great deal more tension than is necessary later. Careño, one of the great pianists of the past, declared it took her years to learn the difference between relaxation and flabbiness, and Paderewski once said to someone, "Sometimes my hand is like a piece of steel, but I do not keep it that way."

In a general way it is better to try to do the thing you have to do loosely, of course, but if that is difficult, try any way to get the effect. The proper looseness can be developed, of course, and that must always be striven for. It is apt to come when you have learned to hold correctly the hand position or mastered difficult fingering. One must not be misled by this—relaxation is important, but it may, like everything else, be overdone.

MEMORIZING

There are many ways of memorizing, and each pupil may select the way that seems most helpful to him. Take your choice, but be sure that you memorize accurately and with certainty.

One of our great pianists has remarked that there are three kinds of musical memory. The first is the kind in which the image of the printed page is retained in the mind, and is seen by the player in his mind's eye. The second is a mechanical memory residing in the fingers, which is proved by the fact that although the player may lose the thread of the composition his fingers continue to play several pages, perhaps, automatically.

The third kind of memory is that which enables a player to sing or hum the composition and actually to go through the mental operation of playing it throughout, after having analyzed and absorbed it so completely that he can reproduce it on his instrument.

"That is the best kind of memory," the pianist said. "That is the kind I possess."

It is unsafe to depend entirely on visualizing the page, or on the automatic memory of fingers. One should literally be able to go through a composition—dynamics, pedaling, and expression—away from the piano, before feeling certain that he has thoroughly grasped it. Memorize it away from the piano if this plan suits you.

Memorize a composition measure by measure, and be able to play any measure by number, if you prefer. This may be your way.

Analyze a composition harmonically, absorb the mood of it, note all the changes in tempo, memorize each hand separately. This last memory exercise is a wonderful help in the fugues of Bach. In fact, a very famous teacher in Chicago used to refuse to listen to a Bach fugue until the pupil had memorized it in this way. This method makes the player much less likely to "fall down" on his piece.

A pupil practicing every day in the same room unconsciously absorbs or memorizes the surroundings and even the looks of the piano. Then, when he plays in other surroundings, he often finds that his memory fails. A great help in settling, or seasoning, a composition in the memory is to practice it hard for a certain length of time and then lay it away. Practice something else. On reviewing the former composition, it will be discovered that something has happened in the memory; the piece has become more firmly a part of the player's mentality. No one knows actually how this comes about; it is one of the mysteries of the mind.

It is usually unsafe to try a composition in public immediately after learning it. It ought to settle, or season, as explained above.

Many a public performer has remarked that no matter how well he knew a concerto or sonata while playing it in his own room, he couldn't feel absolutely sure of it until he had played it in public. Often a weak spot in the memory pops up where it is least suspected.

Get a few friends together and play for them, to test your memory before giving a public performance. Memory is a strange and capricious thing; no one seems able fully to understand it.

Yet consider some of our great orchestra and opera conductors, who play over a symphony on the piano two or three times and then put the score aside forever, or who conduct all of the Wagner operas without scores.

Some pupils have to memorize a piece before they can play it. Others imagine they cannot memorize because they have never earnestly tried. The ability will grow, if cultivated earnestly enough.

DYNAMICS

When we speak of dynamics we mean all the effects produced by varying degrees of power: crescendo, diminuendo, sforzando, marcato (sometimes dependent on rhythm as well), rinforzando (reinforcing, not accenting), fp (forte-piano), or loud and then immediately soft, pf, which is not soft and then loud, as many imagine, but "a little loud," perhaps mezza voce defines it better, and so on. The initials "pf" may indicate many things, but only one thing in music. The initials "mv" (mezza voce), used so often by Brahms, are frequently puzzling to pupils. It is really a term more aptly applied to singing or speaking, but as we try to make the piano sing it has a legitimate place in piano music. Half voice or moderately soft is its meaning.

Remember that diminuendo does not imply a slowing up, nor crescendo a hastening, in tempo. Incalzando (literally, to pursue hotly) may mean both of these, and calando (letting down) may refer to both tone and tempo.

Some composers—Brahms and Grieg, for instance—have a habit of using the terms sostenuto and poco sostenuto when they want to produce the effect of a ritardando. Beethoven uses words like disinvolto (free and gracefully) and sciolto (agile, nimble) that one rarely meets in the works of other composers.

If you wish to play interestingly, pay attention to dynamics, and all other marks, as well. If you don't understand them—look them up. They were usually put in the music by experienced musicians.

Remember that dynamic marks between the two staves apply to both hands, with proper balance of tone relation. The marks above the upper staff refer only to that staff, and those below the lower staff refer to that staff only.

AGOGICS

The term "agogics," or "agogic accents," is often puzzling to pupils and young teachers both. When once explained, however, there is nothing mysterious about it. It belongs in the same field as tempo rubato, and, in fact, no one can play rubato, or espressivo, without making use of agogic emphasis.

A slight prolongation of a note beyond its natural value produces the effect of an emphasis, or accent, without disturbing the regular rhythm, or without being any louder than the surrounding notes. Hugo Riemann, in 1884, first made use of the word, advising that all dynamic variations be combined, with a slight variation in the regularity of the time, in order to complete the expression.

Listen carefully to a fine violinist play something that is written in even notes and you will discover that he slightly holds certain notes, but in a way that does not disturb the flow or movement of the notes. It takes away the ordinary, or elementary, effect, which might otherwise be present. The use of an agogic accent is the only way (without the swell pedal) that one can produce an emphasis on the organ or on any of the keyboard instruments, such as the harpsichord or spinet, where a hard stroke cannot affect the volume of the tone.

REPEATS

Repeats are indicated in various ways. Some of them will be found in old editions only, where several measures are bracketed and the word "bis," above the bracket, indicates that the measures enclosed are to be played twice.

"Bis" is a Latin word which means twice, and in Italian and French theaters the audience makes use of it to obtain a repetition of a number that pleases them. The mark is obsolete for modern editions, but it is well to explain it to pupils. Da capo (literally, from the head, or the beginning) and dal segno (from the sign) are in frequent use, and indicate that the performer is to repeat from the beginning, or from wherever the sign is placed, and play through to the word "fine."

The usual repeat mark is a row of dots placed in the spaces of the staff at the end of a period or section:

Repeats are intended to save paper and printing, and should be observed by the player without losing any time. In other words, the listener is not supposed to realize that there is a repeat mark: the effect should be a continuous flow of music. It is not unusual to hear players hesitate as if trying to decide whether or not to repeat, and often, as a result, a count is lost. The effect is slipshod.

If, at the close of a period to be repeated, a ritardando is found, *don't* observe it the first time; save it for the repeat, for which it is really intended. Don't observe any repeats in playing a da capo. If the repeats are not observed in suites by Bach and Handel, and in Haydn variations, which are built up of short periods to be repeated, it gives the effect of incompleteness, as if the player were only playing half the composition because he was in a hurry to get through.

A few years ago someone started the questionable fad of leaving out all repeats. For a while it obtained quite a following. But observe the great artists, and conductors, and notice if *they* do.

If you are in the audience and can't sit through the repeats, then you are growing old. You had better go home.

When, in a long composition, the repeat covers several pages, there is a reasonable excuse for leaving it out, especially on a long program. If your program contains only a few numbers, play your repeat and try to make it more interesting the second time.

In long Bach arias with a second section, then a long orchestral interlude, then a da capo, it has been found satisfactory to leave out the second section.

THE SHY PUPIL

All teachers, sooner or later, encounter the shy pupil. He seems afraid to let himself out—almost afraid to answer a question. Nowadays, he is described as having an inferiority complex.

The first problem is to determine the cause. Maybe he is overawed by you, his teacher. Talk to him a good deal—perhaps about other things, not his lessons. Give him as much praise as you can, honestly, whenever he does anything well. You can always hold out the promise of something much better if he can overcome his present problems. But don't discuss his shyness. In many subtle ways you can help him to gain more confidence in himself. Make friends with him, in short.

THE OVERCONFIDENT PUPIL

Like the shy pupil, the overconfident one is also a problem, but in a different way. He is the one who is always ready to attempt anything without sufficient preparation; who feels that you don't appreciate his ability; who refuses advice, who always wants to play things that are beyond him; who scorns the classics, and who has no use for serious study.

He is probably the most difficult problem you will meet, but don't let him down with a thump. You may only strengthen his antagonism by such a method.

Try to arrange to have him hear playing that is much superior to anything he is able to do, and make him see the difference. Shame him a little, if possible, though not too much at a time.

Insist on the necessity of his having a good foundation to build on. Make him feel how unreasonable it is, since he has applied for instruction, to take an attitude of superior knowledge. Remember, by constant hammering one is able to wear out a hard rock.

If he does not change over a reasonable period of time, there is probably nothing you can do.

CLASS QUIZZES

Pupils need to have their memories constantly refreshed about the essentials of music. It is not a bad plan to ask them, offhand, what this or that means. In short, at every lesson give them a short quiz. No doubt there will be a roar of objections from teachers.

"Oh, but we don't have time for that!"

The simple answer is—take time for that!

A large number of pupils in schools and conservatories are usually quite floored by any question the least bit out of the ordinary. It is a matter of regret that there is no catechism pertaining to general musical knowledge like that used in the Royal Academy, at London. Every candidate in the Academy must answer the questions before he can qualify for a diploma.

We hear pupils speak of a "pickup note," an "upbeat," and other terms. Ask them the meaning of anacrusis, of ictus, or what is a masculine ending, a feminine ending, or a sequence.

An anacrusis may be a single note or it may be several notes, as in the *Marseillaise*.

Or it may begin soon after the first beat, as in the *Chaconne*, by Durand.

The ictus, as shown, is the initial, or strong, beat in the measure.

A masculine ending is one in which the tonic is approached directly, as again in the *Marseillaise*.

48

There, in the feminine ending, the effect is softened by a suspension before the tonic.

feminine ending

A sequence is a figure either contrapuntal or chordal that moves up or down by degrees, in repetition, like this from the *Messiah*.

SOME DANCE MOVEMENTS—
ANCIENT AND MODERN

The early composers, wishing to produce a concert piece of some length and variety, conceived the idea of stringing together a number of popular dance tunes of the period. They named the result a suite, or, in Italian, a partita.

The suite usually begins with an allemande, which simply means German, a German dance, or movement. Then, for a change, a courante, a saraband, a minuet, or a gavotte was introduced, and the suite almost always was ended by a gigue.

Sometimes Bach began a suite with a prelude, or used two different allemandes or two courantes. The tempo of the allemande was moderate, in two-four or four-four.

The words "courante" (French) and "correnta" (Italian) both mean running, and in music it signifies a fast, lively movement, usually in triple time. In Elizabethan times, the correnta rode on a wave of popularity and was danced on all occasions.

The minuet is of French origin. It is also in triple time and, when danced, the tempo is very stately. A fine example is the minuet in Mozart's *Don Juan,* and the tempo is about one quarter note to 80 M.M. The later minuet, in symphonies, sonatas, and string quartets, is often played faster. Frequently the minuet is paired off with a trio, after which it is repeated alone. Originally, the trio was played by two oboes and a bassoon as a sort of interlude between dances.

The gavotte also came from France and is in common time. It has one peculiarity, however; it always begins on the third beat of the measure, somewhat like an anacrusis. The well-known *Gavotte in B Minor* by Bach begins on the fourth beat of the measure, which puts it out of class. It is really a bourrée, and no one seems to know why it is called a gavotte.

A musette is often paired off with a gavotte, and, as in the case of the trio and minuet, the gavotte is repeated after the musette. The musette gets its name from a similarly called small double-reed wind instrument, possibly of French origin,

50

which produces a drone in the bass, something like a bagpipe. Hence the name of the movement which is built on an organ point.

One is always sure to find a saraband, which is very slow and stately, in the classic suite. The saraband came from Spain, and even today, at the Easter celebration in the cathedral at Seville, boys dance a saraband. Actually, it is scarcely what one would call a dance; it is more like a succession of poses and bows. It is in triple time.

Most classic suites end with a gigue, or jig, a very lively movement in six-eight or twelve-eight time. The tempo must be fast enough to inspire the feet to move. The gigue gets its name from an old bowed instrument upon which it was played.

The pavan, or pavana, is another very solemn and stately dance, in three-four time. The name comes from the word "pavo," which means peacock, and the dance was performed with exaggerated formality and majesty, suggesting the strutting of the bird itself. At the courts of Henry VIII and Francis I this dance was very popular. It was usually followed by a galliard, a much lighter kind of dance than the pavan, and the music was derived from the tune of the pavan.

The passacaglia (Italian), or passacaille (French), is a slow movement in a minor key. It is built on a ground theme, which, according to the rule, must remain in the lower voice. It resembles the chaconne, except that the chaconne is sometimes in a major key, and the ground theme may move into different voices. It is, in a way, a set of variations above a ground theme, but in the chaconne the first and third beats in the measure are accented. Observe this passage in Bach's *Chaconne for Violin.*

Both the passacaglia and the chaconne are in triple time.

Bach's great *Passacaille in C Minor for Organ* is really more like a chaconne because the theme *does* leave the lower voice, and that puts it out of the passacaille class. This dance, like so many others, also originated in Spain, and the derivation of its name is in dispute. It may derive from the words "passo gallo," a rooster step. At any rate, it is proud and stately in character.

The chaconne is probably of Moorish or Arabian origin.

The loure is an old French dance of dignified character, usually in three-four time but sometimes in common time. The second quarter in each measure is dotted.

A tarantella is an exceedingly lively dance that comes from Italy. Its chief characteristic is that it grows increasingly lively toward the end. It is believed by many that the tarantella got its name from the tarantula, a poisonous insect whose bite often results in death. The peasants believed that by dancing and whirling violently, they could work off the poison. Another suggestion is that the dance came from the ancient town of Tarentum. Either theory is plausible but the first explanation seems to agree with the character of the dance. It is usually in six-eight time.

The seguidilla is a rather moderate Spanish dance, in triple time.

The bolero, also a Spanish dance, is in three-four time and is marked by the rhythm ♩ ♫♫ ♫ ♫ with strong emphasis on the first beat. The tempo of the bolero is lively and fascinating. The very popular piece by that name of Ravel's is much too slow in tempo to be national. The rhythms of the bolero and the polonaise are about the same, except that the polonaise is more moderate.

The habanera comes from Havana, Cuba, as its name indicates. It has the same rhythm as the South American Negro dance, the tango, thus ♩. ♫♩♩ | ♩. ♫♩♩ The habanera from the opera *Carmen* is a good illustration of it.

The cachúcha and the jota (hotah) are both very vivacious Spanish dances, in three-four time.

The polonaise, which in translation simply means Polish, is the feminine form of the word, and obviously relates to "la danse," a Polish dance. The Italian name for it is the polacca, and it is in moderate triple time. As noticed above, it is slower than the bolero.

The mazurka, in triple time, is a national Polish dance that ranges from slow to fast, and the third beat in the measure is accented. Chopin wrote fifty-two mazurkas covering a great range of expression and providing a treasure-box of musical thought.

The hopak (gopahk) is a lively obstreperous Russian dance in common time.

The Ländler (meaning: of the country) is a rustic dance in waltz time. It was danced mostly in Bavaria, Bohemia, and Austria. The tyrolienne Swiss dance is very much like it.

In the days of Alessandro Scarlatti, anything that was sung was called a cantata, from the word "cantare," to sing. Anything played on an instrument was a sonata, while a piece for a keyboard instrument was a toccata, from "toccare," to touch.

Through the years, the cantata has come to mean a somewhat extended vocal composition for solos and chorus. And the sonata, through the development of the sonata form, has grown into a composition of not less than two movements and often four. The first movement is written in sonata form, while the slow movement is in free form, and may be in a different key. The last movement is usually in rondo form. Often a scherzo or minuet is introduced. The sonata is the natural outgrowth of the suite, with this difference: a suite is always in the same key, while the movements of a sonata may be in different keys. Chamber music, trios, quartets, quintets, and symphonies are all sonatas in larger form.

The toccata has changed least of all these forms and still remains a brilliant "show-off" piece for a keyboard instrument.

PROGRAM BUILDING

In piano literature especially, we have an almost inexhaustible mass of material from which to select in making programs, so there is no excuse for making a poor one. Good judgment is needed in arranging the different numbers so that each can show its own value, and not "kill" any other or be overshadowed itself, as sometimes happens. Beware of having too many pieces of the same character, or in the same key, in a group together. Contrast them and arrange them exactly as you would flowers or pictures. A succession of pieces in the same mood is not effective.

The conventional program begins with a classic, a prelude and fugue, or several preludes and fugues, preferably in different keys, so as not to tire the ear, then a suite, or partita, an organ toccata, arranged, a Beethoven or Mozart sonata, followed perhaps by a group by Brahms, Schumann, or Chopin. The more modern things are usually placed last. One may prefer to make a one-composer program. If so, there is plenty of contrasting material available without using the best-known things by Schumann or Brahms or Chopin.

Introduce, sometimes, the *Davidsbündlertänze* or *Kreisleriana,* by Schumann; *Pour le Piano,* by Debussy, Moussorgsky's charming and fanciful *Tableaux d'une Exposition,* arranged by Bauer; a group of Godowsky's *Triakontameron,* or Saint-Saëns' op. 72, consisting of six pieces. A piece of chamber music may be used sometimes if the players are available.

Try several historical programs to show the development of music, beginning, of course, with some very early music of the English or Italian schools.

Enthusiastic students will find both pleasure and benefit in arranging a variety of programs, even if they are unable to play them, for program building is an art that must be studied. It doesn't come natural even to many fine players.

Assign to various pupils in the class a program to arrange. Here are some suggestions.

1. A conventional program beginning with an old classic and proceeding to the moderns.

2. A one-composer program.
3. An all-Bach program.
4. A program comprising sets of pieces like Schumann's *Papillons*.
5. A program containing some good themes and variations.
6. A Brahms program.
7. A historical program.

Always stress the importance of contrast in keys and mood. It is not effective to play too many quiet pieces in a row, nor to have pieces in the same key follow each other. Avoid monotony. Valuable experience may be acquired through program building in class, or by bringing in written programs for criticism and discussion.

GOOD TASTE AND HOW TO FORM IT

"No, I wouldn't play it that way. It isn't in good taste."
This remark is frequently heard when several pupils discuss
playing.

What is good taste? Who made it? How can it be acquired?

When one shows good taste (or bad taste), it seems almost as if it were something its possessor was unconscious of,
as in the matter of manners and dress. One recoils instinc-
tively from some things because they offend, or because they
are too conspicuous, or too blatant, or not harmonious. Perhaps it is impossible to define good taste or to place it within
boundaries, for sometimes what is bad taste to one individual
does not offend another. Good taste in musical art must em-
brace all that is best in tradition, which is, after all, but a
composite of all the good taste of the past, as well as what
our most reliable artists of today consider the best.

It can best be acquired by listening only to the best we
have, and by consulting constantly the best authorities for
information, and by gathering and sifting out the best, always.

You may make mistakes but you can correct them.

Be careful not to copy the failures of other artists, especially eccentric movements, or a tremolo (in singing).

A certain great recitalist tells the story of a young adorer
who studied all the records of the artist obtainable. She finally had a chance to sing for the artist herself, only to discover that she had copied all of her idol's failings and none
of her virtues.

"Too bad, poor girl! She learned all of my faults," the
artist commiserated. Those who really possess good taste are
always a minority—all the more reason to strive earnestly to
rank among the few.

ONE-SIDED PREFERENCES IN
MUSICAL INTERESTS

One sometimes encounters a musician who seems to have absolutely no interest outside of his own branch of art, who cares nothing for a piano recital, who doesn't like a string quartet, who is bored by a violin or cello recital, and to whom an opera, an orchestra, or a fine choir is a thing of indifference. This is all wrong.

Many of our finest singers have been good pianists: Melba, Sembrich, Galli-Curci, and Nordica, among others. In fact, to this accomplishment they probably owe much of their success as singers.

Pianists, too, ought to like good singing; and they should study it to enable them to "sing" their melodies in their playing.

Organists should be good pianists in order to be better organists. A prominent organist in Rome says that he always learns organ music on the piano before trying it on the organ.

There are people who like nothing later than Haydn; and there are others who find Beethoven too old-fashioned for use. Good musicianship implies a broad, well-rounded knowledge and appreciation of all forms of music. In the United States we have increasingly good advantages to study and hear opera and fine choirs. The radio brings the best orchestra concerts into our living rooms.

Teachers should strive to inspire in their pupils a desire to seek everything in music that is good and worthy. "Try to grasp things beautiful" is the motto of Phi Kappa Lambda Honor Society.

QUEER MANNERISMS

Unconscious habits can easily spoil the effect of good playing for the listener. Avoid bobbing the head, "ducking," making faces, working the mouth, swaying, throwing the hands too high, crouching, rolling from side to side, making a noise with the pedals, grunting, and humming. A certain amount of freedom of motion is allowable and desirable, but the teacher must not hesitate, tactfully, of course, to correct unnecessary and exaggerated habits, as they are often unsuspected by the pupil himself.

Many a good performance or recital has been adversely criticized not for the playing but because of some eccentricity or annoying habit of the artists. The day has gone by when a player or conductor could rely on long hair or strange movements for success.

On the other hand, care should be taken not to appear too stiff or awkward. The teacher should be the judge.

PRACTICE

Practice. That one word sums it all up. It is the whole thing in a nutshell, and yet to contain what can be said about practice would require a nutshell the like of which has never been created.

When you have taught a pupil how to get the most out of an hour's practice, you have given him the thing of greatest value in music study.

The difference between an hour's practice by the clock and an hour of really concentrated work at the piano is very great, yet many pupils do not realize this distinction and have a very dim idea of what it really means to work hard. For one thing, it means to become so absorbed that one doesn't realize where one is or what time it is. One often hears the lofty remark that it is unnecessary to work long, hard hours if one concentrates. Be assured that a great deal of both concentration and hard work are needed.

You may have the finest teachers available; you may boast that you pay fifty dollars an hour for lessons, and yet if you don't work you will not be able to get very far.

Your teacher may advise you, explain to you, illustrate for you, but he cannot work for you. Bear that in mind! How often we think we have mastered a difficult passage only to find, the next day, that it has "gone back" or got out of the fingers, and has to be learned all over again!

Of course, every time we relearn it, we are driving the nail a little deeper.

There is a story told about one of our most beloved pianists who, while staying in a Boston hotel, kept practicing, always practicing. A lady who had a room nearby, became curious to know how many times he repeated the same passage. Finally, one day, she decided to keep count. To her amazement, she discovered that he played the same passage over nine hundred times!

The same pianist, working with the left hand only on several measures of the Beethoven sonata op. 31, kept a visitor waiting nearly an hour. Finally, growing a little restless, the visitor excused himself, saying he would take a walk and come back later. When he returned, an hour later, the practicer was still going strong on the same few measures. The visitor jokingly asked, "Why work so hard? You could easily fool the public." The pianist replied, "Yes, so I could. However, I still have a conscience."

One of our great Viennese pianists is said to have practiced all day long for a couple of weeks on several pages of the left-hand part of a difficult composition by Liszt.

When our great pianists practice like this, what are we to learn? The lesson is this: the purpose of practicing is not to put in time, but to set out to accomplish, with determination, the task in hand. Many repetitions there must be, but never let them become "meaningless repetitions." As a teacher, your duty is to show the pupil how best to accomplish what he has undertaken, rather than merely assign him a lot of material and tell him to go ahead.

Let us see if we can arrive at some understanding of what good practice means.

First of all, don't keep looking at the clock. Don't keep wishing you had some place to go, or that someone would come along and talk to you. You must fix every part of your attention on what you are doing. If you have really made up your mind to work, then organize, plan. and resolve to get lots of fun out of doing it—and it can be fun—and in a few weeks you will be astonished at your progress. There is scarcely anything you can't achieve with time and determination.

Generally speaking, it is wise for the young practicer to divide practice time systematically—so much time for purely technical work, setting-up exercises, scales and arpeggios, and so much time for sonatas, pieces, and so on. In this way he is less likely to forget or neglect something. This is especially important when one has only a limited amount of time.

Always try to have some technical problem to be worked out, something that at first seems impossible. Work at it very slowly at first, for even the most difficult things may be easy in a very slow tempo. Pay close attention to the fingering, the muscular action, the position, and the other necessary things. Then, day by day, add a little speed.

If the problem is one of rhythm, don't let it go as soon

as you think you have mastered it; keep on until the rhythmic pattern in the sound of the notes suggests at once to your mind the way it looks on paper. Absorb it so completely that you can do it almost unconsciously. The lack of the ability to decipher rhythms instantly is the reason many players are poor sight-readers.

If there are difficulties for both hands at the same time, then learn each hand alone and put them together slowly. Never be satisfied until you know and can explain clearly, exactly where each note belongs in relation to the count and in relation to the other notes in the measure.

Slow practice is excellent, but it is not a panacea, or cure-all. Sometimes you must learn to go fast.

In slow practice, listen to every single note for quality, volume, and tone.

Most players seem to find it better to practice a composition exactly as they intend to play it in public. Others seem to prefer to approach a performance from slow practice. However, the other way seems more reasonable.

Nearly all the great pianists have some favorite exercises they use to get in trim. Although some declare they never practice, do not believe them.

To the student, the fourth and fifth fingers offer a never-ending problem, and something ought to be done every day to help produce equality of strength and agility in these two weak members.

Don't waste time practicing over and over something that is not difficult. Seek out the difficulties in a composition that is new to you, and learn those first. They may be a few measures for the left hand, or something in skips or chords; master them, and the rest is easy.

There is a kind of practicer who, when he makes a mistake, starts at the beginning again and more often than not repeats the same mistake in the same place. This is plainly a waste of time. Try to discover what the trouble is. If it is bad fingering, stay right with it until the trouble is cleared up, then go back and connect it with the rest of the piece.

When one habitually misses a certain note in a passage, a good way to become certain of it is to go just as far as that note and stop there, again and again. If you play a flat instead of a natural, think about it—even say aloud, "B, not B flat." If it is caused by wrong fingering, correct it, and then, as you approach it again, be alert.

Practice a scale or arpeggio or passage figure in the reverse direction, with the same fingering. This is one of the quickest ways to clear up a difficulty. Transpose it into another key. Change the rhythm in every conceivable way. Accent it very strongly, much more than you intend to play it in performance. Learn it with a different fingering, if practicable. Some may object that this may result in a confusion in fingering. It won't if you have thoroughly mastered the first fingering. If you know several roads to London, you are not likely to get lost on your way there.

There are many little tricks in practicing that the teacher who is experienced can pass on to the student, but which he might not discover for himself, in years. Pass them on.

Make it a rule never to let anything on the page go by without understanding it. Always have questions to ask—any musical term, or sign, or effect that you do not understand. Find out, if you do not know!

Use imagination in practice. Try shading your scales and technics. Learn to make a steady, gradual crescendo over a longer stretch. The usual mistake is to begin too loud and arrive at the climax too soon. You have wasted ammunition, if you do this.

Practice finger staccato with the hand held still and the action from the knuckle joint. If persevered in, in a short time this will work wonders with a heavy, bungling touch. If you doubt this, just give it a trial!

One must be prepared to use the touch that is next to legato, variously described as portamento (carrying), legato-staccato, or negative staccato, as Scharwenka called it. Those notes that have a dot over them and those dots covered by a slur should receive three fourths of their actual value, according to all authorities who have explained the rules for touch.

Portamento is probably the best name for this touch, as we literally carry the length over beyond what we would if only the dot were there. Notice that, on the piano, the effect is not nearly so distinctive as it is on the clavichord and the harpsichord, although it is still effective on the piano in slow playing. In velocity, it is impossible and is never indicated.

Pupils must be taught to use the different touches where they are appropriate, in order to make their playing interesting and varied. The player who has only one touch is like an engine that runs on only one cylinder!

Try to understand a composition, etude, or sonata in as many different ways as possible by becoming thoroughly acquainted with the material contained in it. If you practice in one way only, you are like a person who passes some great cathedral every day without seeing anything but the front of it. What idea of it can such a person have? He should examine the sides, the transepts, the apse; go inside and look at the arches, the chapels, the altar; examine the windows; go up in the tower and look down; try to determine the style of the architecture—in sum, thoroughly explore it. Even then there will be a great deal that he has missed.

Brahms was once asked what he thought it took to make a musician. He answered, "Only three things. The first thing is work; the second is work; and the third is more work!"

When one hand becomes tired, give it a rest and use the other a while. Muscles develop only through exercise and by becoming tired. We literally tear down muscle tissue when we work hard, and then the blood contributes new material and builds it up again, each time a little stronger. The main thing is not to tear down too much tissue at once. If your muscles hurt or ache, rub them in the direction of the heart (that is, don't rub the fingers toward the points), and assist nature to dispose of the waste material, which is causing the discomfort.

Let us take for a lesson one measure of four notes from Plaidy, intended to be repeated any number of times.

Let us first play it with the right hand, raising the fingers a good deal and playing very strongly.

Now let us play it so:

then so:

Now play it the same way with the left hand. Now play it with the hands together doing exactly the same thing with both hands. Now play it with one hand doing even legato eighths and the other the accents and rhythms in the illustrations; then reverse the hands. Now let one hand play finger staccato, while the other plays perfect legato. Now reverse. Now take the same figure of one measure and repeat it three times, playing it in triplets, with the accents well brought out.

This is not easy as it requires very close attention, but it stimulates concentration and makes the pupil think. If he doesn't, he cannot do it. Now imagine the same figure as if written in quarter notes:

then eighths:

then triplets of eighths:

then sixteenths:

Be careful to keep the same tempo for the quarter-note value throughout.

Now let us try something more puzzling. It is assumed that the pupil has learned to play these different lessons one at a time. Of course, it would be foolish to do them all at the beginning. It may take several lessons to get the different hand combinations going smoothly. Let us now try both hands together on the same figure, but let us play the right hand, to start with, in triplets, and the left in figures of two notes. Both must be perfectly even, and therein lies the puzzle. Too few pupils ever acquire the ability to do this easily. They play them after a fashion, but not evenly. Let us take them *very slowly,* thus:

Now try it in reverse.

If you count evenly and play the note on the count indicated, it can't easily go wrong. Lose no opportunity of applying this rhythm principle to technical studies until the pupil finally can play them easily and correctly; then he may try playing four notes in one hand against three notes in the other. There ought to be a steady development in the pupil's ability to think rhythms and compound rhythms. The great danger lies in not getting enough rhythm drill. There is little danger of becoming too proficient.

Don't forget, as you go along, to try to make a few shadings—a good crescendo and diminuendo. Even try practicing one hand loud and the other soft, at the same time. It must ultimately be accomplished, so why not try it? So often these things are left to the dim future and consequently remain there.

Remember to keep a steady, even tempo in practicing. Of course, we don't always play in strict time, but we must be able to when occasion demands it, and no one can make an intelligent time variation until he is able to keep absolutely strict time. Watch the rests and give them their full time. Don't cut corners.

Perhaps by now the pupil will begin to see the difference between hard study and mere practicing. Teach him as early as possible not to shirk. The teacher, of course, must have infinite patience with the pupil and continually suggest different things to do as one thing has been learned. The study of technique *need not be dull.*

Suppose your pupil has difficulty getting his fingers on the keys in a passage like this:

Have him play it thus:

then

Add different variants as the study progresses. Any one of them is likely to be found in one composition or another, and when the student encounters one again he will find little difficulty in playing it. Absolute accuracy of time must be kept. A general failing among students is to give dotted notes less time than they should have, which results in a slipshod rhythm.

The student should be constantly occupied with some difficult problem to be worked out, something that at first seems impossible of solution. But, of course, nothing is impossible. With patience and determination, he will master the difficulty. There is no better way to develop technique.

Here are ten good suggestions on the subject of practicing:

1. Keep a steady tempo.
2. Have each hand do a different thing, such as playing the left hand very loud and the right hand soft. Then try the reverse.

3. Play the right hand, even, against the left hand, dotted. Reverse.

4. Play one hand staccato against legato in the other hand.

5. Try reversing the direction of a passage, using the same fingering.

6. If one hand or arm becomes disabled, don't go to bed and give up work. There is always the other hand, and it may be your chance to develop your left hand.

7. Get used to transposing passages, first in nearby keys and later into more remote keys. Most likely you will have to learn a new fingering. That will be good for you.

8. Spend a good deal of time practicing uneven rhythms together. Pischna, nos. 1 and 2, may be arranged so that the right hand plays two rhythms, for instance, the thumb and second finger play two notes against triplets in the fourth and fifth, while the left hand plays four notes, and sometimes even eight. They must be accurate. Then reverse it, playing the triplets between the thumb and second finger. Then make the left hand do what the right hand did. This means work, but it is the kind of thing you may be called upon to do in playing difficult compositions.

9. Never lose sight of what is back of all the technique, rhythms, mechanism, and so on, which are only a means to an end. That end is the music, the soul of the whole thing. Technique may be compared to means of transportation. It is the conveyance that gets you somewhere.

10. Learn something for the left hand alone. It gives a feeling of independence that can be acquired in no other way. Try Saint-Saëns' *Bourrée,* or *Gigue,* in op. 135, or Scriabin's *Prelude and Nocturne,* or Reger's *Four Left Hand Studies,* or even Tchaikovsky's arrangement of *Perpetual Motion* by Weber. You will not be sorry if you learn to play them well.

EXPRESSION

When we speak of expression, a number of questions immediately jump to mind.

Just what does it mean, literally speaking?

How many kinds of expression are there?

How is expression accomplished?

How does dynamic expression differ from what we understand as "espressivo"?

Should all music be played espressivo?

What do we understand by the term "espressivo"?

Is there danger of overloading music with expression?

When should it not be employed?

What do composers mean by the following terms: "senza espressione," "molto" or "assai espressivo," "poco espressione"?

What sort of music is naturally in the expressive style?

Is there any music so beautiful and complete in itself that it needs no help from you, except that you play it with good tone, good rhythm, in fact, so perfect that you can add nothing to it?

The dictionary definition of the word is "the outward manifestation of some interior feeling, emotion, or sentiment. To express, to bring out. To manifest what is inside."

But in order to know how to do this, there are many tangible auxiliaries that have to be studied, learned, and applied. Now, someone is going to say that expression, to be good, must be the natural outpouring of the soul. Yes, indeed! How true that is! But observe the large number of people who have strong feelings and cannot express them because they lack an adequate vocabulary and the art of oratory. They just don't know how to say what they want to say. Here is an exact parallel. The words and the phrases must all be learned first; then a natural outpouring of ideas may be expected. People who have a command of words usually succeed in expressing exactly what they mean.

At first, most pupils are quite in the dark as to your meaning if you say to them: "More expression. Put your soul into it. Play more as you feel." These commands mean very little to them until the teacher gives them a concrete example. Play a passage from a Beethoven adagio or largo once in perfectly strict, square time; then play the same passage with the treatment it deserves, and ask the pupil if he sees any difference.

Dynamic expression is a foregone conclusion; it is always in good taste, even in something martial, which depends on its rhythm, and where espressivo would be out of place.

When we play with expression, we take some liberties with the time—prolong certain notes beyond their exact value, stretch the time, so to speak, make it elastic. It is akin to rubato. If a pupil has absolutely no natural instinct for expression, there is reason to doubt that he ever can learn it well enough to make it sound natural. He may be taught to accomplish it by imitation, but it can scarcely be a real out-pouring of feelings if the feelings do not exist. Still, there is the question: Is there really ever such a pupil? Don't be too quick in deciding! Many pupils have the feeling hidden deep down, but have no idea how to bring it out. With such pupils there is always hope.

There are certain tricks (if one may use the word) of expression that can be learned, and used discreetly, like play-ing a chord, an interval, or an octave arpeggiato, in order to get the effect of expansiveness, which is so much more diffi-cult to produce on the piano than with wind or string instru-ments. The lower bass note may sometimes be sounded a trifle in advance of the other parts for the same effect, but be careful not to use this effect too often. When it becomes a habit or mannerism, it is abominable, and should be dis-couraged. Who has not heard a player who breaks a chord or interval with such regularity that you know it is coming? You watch for it, and you lose the feeling of the music! You wish he wouldn't do it. Save those effects for a very special occasion.

Remember to taper off your cadences—the resolving note softer than the first, which is always allowed an emphasis. Music that is intended to express restlessness, rage, or any kind of strong excitement is often marked appassionato, and implies a rushing tempo and strong accents. Since we have mentioned this word, please remember that it has no "sh" sound. Say "appasseeonahto," not "appashonato." Music intended to represent a calm mood may be marked piacevole, tranquillo, or sostenuto, and it is well to pay attention to these marks in order to produce the right effect.

Sometimes, even in compositions of very stormy character, there comes a lyric phrase, one which suggests a song, and is marked con espressione, or espressivo, or sostenuto. Then relax the tempo suitably. You may make important notes a little longer than their true value, combine with a little more tone to increase the effect, as

Try to give a curve to such a phrase to make it say something musical. It is more natural to increase in tone in the ascending passages and to diminish in a descending direction, although this should not always be done.

Remember, when the same phrase is repeated several times, you must try to treat it in a variety of ways, to avoid monotony. If you give it a good deal of expression the first time it occurs, then give it less the second time. The question then arises: Wouldn't it be in better taste not to express too much at first and to save something for later?

It is much safer for the young player to have all these effects prearranged and decided, because if left to the impulse of the moment the result is often unsatisfactory. A more experienced player may be trusted to take a risk, but even then he sometimes does something he didn't intend.

Don't use excessive expression. The result may sometimes be ludicrous. Enough but not too much is the golden rule here. Don't imitate the idiosyncrasies of some noted artists, by rolling on the piano bench, crouching, or gazing upward. Such things are not expression; they are mannerisms, and are apt to be annoying and distracting.

A lady who was studying singing at a conservatory in Berlin once got into a heated discussion about expression. "Too much expression? Impossible! Ridiculous! One must express everything! Let the feelings out!" Such was the way she thought about it. A little while later she sang at a small recital *Oh! Wie wunderschön ist die Frühlingszeit!* She rolled her eyes, swayed her body, and wagged her head to such a degree that the whole class was soon giggling. Her excess of expression had defeated its purpose.

The introduction to Mendelssohn's *Rondo Capriccioso* may easily be made to sound sentimental and, so to speak, "dawdling," by playing it too expressively. Both Mendelssohn and Moszkowski strongly objected to having too much liberty taken with the time in their compositions; they probably realized the effect would be an absurd exaggeration. Pieces of a certain type should be performed senza (without) espressione, as they are frequently marked. The *Rondo* just mentioned is a streak of velocity and leaves little chance for expressive playing. In this, dynamic expression is certainly in order.

Earlier pianists, as well as singers, were not expected to put much soul into their performance, as the prevailing style demanded brilliant cadenzas, sparkling runs, and, of course, beautiful tone. Nor did their training qualify them for reaching the deeper meanings of music.

Beethoven was the wonder and admiration of his contemporaries because, they said, he played slow movements quite as well as brilliant and rapid ones. It is much more difficult to play an adagio well than to play an allegro. A great many different effects are at the disposal of the player. Study them well and learn to use them suitably in the music you perform.

Here are fifteen pointers that, if thoroughly assimilated, can help improve expression:

1. Establish a good balance of tone between the two hands.
2. Determine where the climax of the phrase is to be.
3. Shade or taper off a cadence or short phrase.
4. Follow dynamics indicated unless absolutely certain you have a better plan.
5. Use agogics.
6. Sometimes intensify the big note of the phrase by delaying it, or by hesitating slightly before playing it. Make a slight tenuto on it.
7. Play a chord, an interval, or an octave arpeggio to gain expansiveness, but use it sparingly.
8. On rare occasions, sound the lower bass note a little

in advance of the right hand, likewise to gain expansiveness.

9. In cases where it is appropriate, the approach to a grand climax may be hurried for effect. Composers sometimes mark these passages stringendo, affrettando, stretto, or accelerando. Again, you may find "senza" or "con" in connection with these terms.

10. The normal thing in approaching a hold, or fermata, is to prepare the hold by a ritardando, and to make a slight pause after the hold before continuing. This has grown out of the fact that singers and players of wind instruments must have a chance to take breath. It has become the normal thing to do. Sometimes both the ritardando and the pause are disregarded for special effects.

11. Be sure to establish a correct tempo. A fine composition may be obscured and its performance botched by a tempo too slow or too fast, as the case may be. Widor used to say that the fastest notes in a piece must be considered in establishing the tempo, for if you are obliged to slow down for them it sounds as if the piece were too difficult for you. Perhaps it is not going too far to assume that for every composition there is a certain tempo in which it sounds most effective and natural. The listener who knows will soon discover the difference. The personal preferences of composers should be observed. Mendelssohn liked a fast tempo, and his presto and molto allegro are about speed limit.

12. When a passage or phrase is repeated, try to play it differently the second time—a different plan of expression or a very slight change in tempo. A little goes a great way. In sections or periods of the Bach suites and partitas that are marked for repeat, and also those marked for ritard at the end of the section, remember that the ritard comes on the repeat, *not* the first time through. Short repeats such as these should be observed; otherwise the composition is bound to sound fragmentary and incomplete.

13. On the piano, a long note must have more tone than the short notes. Even in pianissimo playing, a note

that is to last a measure must have enough tone to carry through; if not, the effect is thin and empty. The other notes in the measure must keep to pianissimo. This is the nature of the piano; some may like to consider it a fallacy, but there it is.

14. When one voice comes to a standstill on a long note, that is the chance for the other voices to come forward and be as interesting as they can. On the piano, after the long note is struck, it can produce no further effect, of course.

15. Embellishments in slow movements—largo, adagio, lento, and such—should be played in the character of the movement, and not crisp or snappy, as they would be in a fast movement. Embellishments, as a rule, should be played on a slightly lower dynamic plane.

INTERPRETATION

Interpretation means bringing out the meaning of a composition, preferably the meaning intended by the composer. If it is given unusual values, it still is interpretation, but perhaps not altogether good. There is such a thing as false interpretation. Needless to say, the player's technique, and his command of all means of expression, must be adequate before he can hope to really interpret the composition.

First, try to understand the mood of the composition, and generally the name will be a great help. If it relates to history or a locality, find out all you can about it. One must have a mental picture of it. Take a tarantelle, for example. If this dance originated in Tarentum, as some suppose, the circumstance is of far less imaginative value than if we can picture it as being danced by someone who has been bitten by a tarantula, and is trying to expel the poison of the bite by engaging in this rapid whirling dance, which becomes more and more furious toward the end.

A gavotte or minuet recalls the stiff dress and courtly manners of the period when it was in vogue, and it must be rhythmic.

Many of Bach's fugues express something very tangible. In Book I of *The Well-Tempered Clavier,* the second fugue in C minor is as grotesque and full of monkeyshines as anything can possibly be. A little further along, the one in D major conjures up a picture of a procession of fat priests with banners, marching solemnly and pompously. The one in B flat minor, both the prelude and the fugue, evokes the solemn atmosphere of a church, with colored windows and organ tones. The C sharp major prelude has a joy and vivacity that is highly infectious, and the fugue, a geniality that recalls the smile of *Frau* Schumann-Heink.

The popular story connected with Beethoven's *Moonlight Sonata* is no doubt a great aid to its interpretation for many students who would otherwise see little in it.

Bird songs about the nightingale, the lark, or a prophetic bird all supply an idea for interpretation. In Schubert's song, *The Trout,* needless to say, the little sextolet figure in the

74

bass suggests the darting about of the trout in the water—and alas for fingers that are not agile enough to dart over the keys as quickly!

Moussorgsky's oxcart piece in *Pictures at an Exhibition* portrays the steady, plodding gait of the oxen, and if it is played either lightly or too fast it is denatured, so to speak.

In the slow movement of Saint-Saëns' *Trio in F Major* you must imagine the lumbering stride of camels across the desert, and the bells that jingle on their harness. Young pupils may often be interested and helped in playing sonatas and sonatinas by describing the old instruments for which they were written, the spinet, the clavichord, and the harpsichord. Tell them about the instruments and about the composers who wrote for them. Few pupils know anything about them. Tell them about Handel practicing on the harpsichord at midnight in his attic; about Bach laboriously copying by moonlight the music that he so much wished to possess; about Mozart walking over the organ pedals when he was too small to reach them from the bench. In the minds of many pupils these names are simply names on paper—and right here let us remark that to be able to tell your pupils such things you must know them yourself.

Interpretation cannot be achieved without great pains. Opera singers, to better interpret the roles they are to sing, have been often known to visit the scenes where the operas are located to observe the costumes and manners and gestures of the people living there: Seville for *Carmen,* Paris for *Bohème,* Rome for *Tosca,* and so on. The most exhaustive research is undertaken in matters of costume and customs, in order to give the right picture.

The same old question always arises in regard to the old classics—Scarlatti, Turini, Paradisi, and Bach. Shall I try to play them in the style of the epoch, or shall I make a big thundering modern piece out of them, since instruments and ideas have changed since they were written? It may help you to choose if you will listen to Miss Hess or *Herr* Gieseking play a Scarlatti sonata and note their crystalline clarity and dainty velocity. No mistake can be made in following their example. There is no thunder, no excessive use of pedal, but instead, a most exquisite lightness and an amazing velocity. It is not easy to do, but try it, anyway.

IMAGINATION IN PLAYING

As early as possible one must try to get away from the idea of notes and get into the realm of effects, for that is what music really is—effects. The notes are simply a means to an end—just like any other material out of which something is constructed. We must inject something, some idea, some thought, into the music, or we are very likely to get nothing out of it when all is done.

If the composition admits of it at all, try to fit some idea or picture to it. Try to supply some words that will help to bring out the meaning of the phrase.

Even a finger study of a rapid, light character may be made more interesting by supplying it with some such conception as chasing butterflies, or playing hide-and-seek, and then playing it with the motions of these actions in mind. After a little practice, the mechanism seems to fade and the idea comes out.

Someone has said that a person who has not ridden in a gondola in Venice cannot possibly play a barcarolle as it should be played. That may be going too far, but surely the reason that many barcarolles are a succession of mechanical rhythms, instead of the rock and swing of a boat and the ripple of the waves, is because the pupil does not understand what a barcarolle means.

This is where the teacher can be of use. He must be able to stir the imagination with a little romance, to form a picture that the pupil can visualize and then try to reproduce in effect. Suppose we take Grieg's lovely *Notturno in C Major* as an example. Surely Grieg never filled four pages with more exquisite beauty. It is divinely lovely!

You may form your own picture. Here is one that may serve. If it doesn't happen to be yours, no matter. First, let us find out what the pupil understands by the title *Notturno,* as Grieg called it in Italian. Something to do with evening or night. The Germans call it *Nachtstück,* or nightpiece, the mood inspired by night. This nightpiece is quiet and peaceful throughout. Let us picture a lovely flower garden with lilac bushes in bloom. It is evening, of course. The quiet triplet movement in the left hand may suggest some of the rhythms in nature—the movement of the leaves in the breeze—whatever you like, but it is quiet. The melody in the right hand, in even eighth notes, sways and rises a little, now and then, with the wind.

Suddenly the warble of a bird in the lilac bush is heard, and those who have never actually heard one may be excused for not knowing that it is a nightingale. Then another nightingale sings in a little higher key, a little beyond. Now begins a tremendous surge, but it must not be a storm, though it reaches a big climax. It begins very softly. Let us imagine the moon slowly emerging from behind the clouds and flooding everything with glory. But the moonlight shines for a short time only, then it begins to fade, and we are taken back hesitatingly to where we were at the beginning.

Some may prefer to imagine a strong breeze starting up and swaying the treetops. Think of it in any way you like; so long as you *think*.

Soon the nightingale sings again, then a measure of breathless silence falls as we listen. Has he gone? No—wait! There on a distant branch, at the foot of the garden, he sings again, a good night. Then we have three simple but wonderful chords, which must rise and sway and settle down to silence in C major, and the picture is ended. Don't take the pedal off too soon. Allow this peaceful chord to fade out gradually. You can easily spoil the picture you have created by stopping too abruptly. Try to hold your listeners.

Now, one of two things is possible: either Grieg meant something lovely and poetic by this piece, or he meant absolutely nothing but a succession of notes. Can there be any argument?

Some of the Chopin nocturnes suggest a tremendous emotional storm; for instance, the dramatic C sharp minor, the first part of which is frequently played too fast, and the one in C minor. The F sharp major nocturne is full of sighs and gasps, and the one in D flat major, sobs and entreaties.

Sgambati's B minor nocturne contains a tremendous storm in the middle part, and its ending is one of the loveliest to be found in any composition in this category. Schumann's

In der Nacht is full of wraiths and ghostly swirls. The rich nocturne literature is highly imaginative and full of images to be evoked.

Put something into them, or you surely will get but little out of them. If you go too far, you may be called sentimental; if you can succeed in going just far enough, you may be called poetic.

Here is a brief list of compositions and their composers that are exceptionally useful to illustrate imagination in playing. Parenthetically, after some of them, are comments on what they suggest.

Raff	*La Fileuse* (A girl spinning)
Godard	*Pan* (The god Pan playing his pipe)
"	*The Swallows* (Darting, swirling flight of birds)
Sternberg	*Sulla Laguna* (A boat ride on the lagoon)
Pierné	*Cache-cache* (Hide and seek)
Rheinberger	*The Chase* (A hunting piece— horns)
Grieg	*Nocturne in C Major* (See above)
Debussy	*Doctor Gradus* (Someone practicing a Clementi study)
"	*The Sunken Cathedral*
"	*Claire de Lune*
"	*Reflections in the Water*
"	*Garden in the Rain*
"	*The Little Shepherd*
Philipp	*The Elf* (Skipping, jumping)
"	*Claire de Lune* (Moonlight)
Borodin	*Au Couvent* (Chiming of deep-voiced bells)
Moszkowski	*The Juggleress* (Tossing balls in the air)
Scharwenka	*Erzählung* (Story or legend)
Saint-Saëns	*The Swan* (Gliding motion)
Schumann	*Warum* (The eternal question)
"	*Hunting Song,* op. 28
"	*Prophetic Bird* (What does he foretell?)

"	*Verrufene Stelle* (A haunted place)
"	*Carnaval,* op. 9
"	*Viennese Carnival Pranks,* op. 26
Grieg	*March of the Dwarfs,* op. 54
Gurlitt	*Butterflies,* op. 158
Liszt	*Gondoliera*
MacDowell	*The Eagle* (Soaring, floating; bird in the air)
"	*Moonlight*
"	*To a Water Lily*
Goossens	*Kaleidoscope*
Tchaikovsky	*By the Fireside*
"	*Troika Ride* (Three-horse team— sleigh bells)
"	*Hunting Song*
"	*The Reapers* (Steady sweep of mowers)
"	*Harvest*

CHARACTERISTICS OF
DIFFERENT COMPOSERS

The conscientious piano teacher will bring to the attention of his pupils the characteristics that distinguish the music of different composers so that they may learn how the music of each should sound when it is played.

Scarlatti, one of the earliest Italian composers, wrote for delicate instruments on which speed, lightness and nimble fingers were of the utmost importance. His music demands a kind of technique that is difficult for pupils to attain without years of practice. Nevertheless, they must study his charming little pieces and keep the ideal before them always. One finds almost no octaves unless in some arrangement. For Paradisi, Turnini, Porpora, and all the rest of the early Italian composers, the same thing is required—extreme agility, not a great deal of soul, and an elegant style, of course. The pupil must listen to and study the performance of the greatest pianists.

Mozart might be called the apostle of daintiness, both in his songs and in his piano music. A certain ingenuous sincerity joined with perfect finger control for the crystalline runs and trills (every note a pearl) is needed to play it well. The player who thumps Mozart should be put in jail. Mozart is not like the early Italians, without passionate expression. The A minor sonata, which is said to show the influence of Handel, was written by Mozart at the time his friends were insisting that he go to Paris. He did not want to go, and worried about it. The last movement expresses a desperate, almost fretful, mood of impatience and worry.

Velocity is needed. It is scarcely possible to play the last movement of the *Sonata No. 7 in F Major* too fast, provided every note is heard distinctly.

Study several of his twenty-eight piano concertos if you wish to test your fluency. They are not easy. Why is it we hear so few pianists play Mozart as we wish to hear it?

Haydn and Clementi belong so nearly to the same period as Mozart that the same things may be said in regard to them. Haydn left us many good sonatas, though not many piano concertos. When the time has arrived, one can derive much benefit from the study of Clementi's excellent etudes.

Mendelssohn loved fast tempi and scintillating execution. He must have realized that the character of his music was such that when the expressive side was overdone it easily became sentimental and too "sweetish." He often wrote senza espressione and objected strongly to having ritardandos where he had not written them. It is a pity that many players sentimentalize the introduction to the *Rondo Capriccioso* by overdoing the expression. The *Rondo* is a streak of velocity.

Many musicians pretend to despise Mendelssohn's music as too old-fashioned to play. Surely this is not true of all of it. The *Concerto in G Minor,* if delightfully played, is exciting and pleasant to listen to, and very useful for study. The charming little *Etude in F Major,* op. 104, as played by Rachmaninoff, is exquisite. It is all in the way it is played. It is music that is extremely well suited to the piano. The violin concerto is a standby.

Chopin is supposed to have believed it impossible to equalize the strength of the fingers, so he tried, in writing, to spare the weak fingers and throw the burden on the naturally strong fingers. As a result he produced the most "pianistic" music. It doesn't follow that great strength is not necessary to play Chopin. It *is* necessary. One must be able to embellish singing melodies with cadenzas of vaporous lightness. Sometimes thunderous octaves are necessary. One must be able to reproduce the legato of the violin and of the best singers. One must be a master of rubato. And one must be able to tell a story in the ballades.

The etudes, beside being gems of beauty, provide the most exhaustive study for execution. No concert program seems complete without a few of them. It is possible that the time may come when people will abandon them as being too old-fashioned, but that time is certainly a long way off.

Liszt left the well-known path and tried to make the piano sound like an orchestra. He arranged throbbing tremolo passages for the right hand and left hand, and thundering blind octave and chord effects. The noise that he produced at first horrified his listeners and created two distinct factions: one pronounced him vulgar and blatant; the other saw something new and tremendous in him and believed in his genius. Perhaps in some things he is still vulgar, but those have died a natural death. His arrangements of songs by Schubert, Schumann, and others are considered excellent. His *Hark, Hark the Lark* cannot be excelled. His *Concerto in E Flat* and Tchaikovsky's in B flat minor are the great show concertos for great pianists. He knew how to be quiet and idyllic in his smaller pieces such as *Au Bord d'une Source,* which seems as near to nature as it is possible for piano music to be. He certainly broadened the technical outlook for the world, as Chopin also did.

Who can describe what it takes to play Beethoven and Brahms well? First of all, a noble conception and familiarity with all that is great in architecture, painting, sculpture, and life, is called for. A good technique is a foregone conclusion, but not exactly the Liszt or Chopin kind. Much of Beethoven's piano music is not "pianistic." His was an orchestral mind, and he thought for orchestra even in writing for piano. He could crash and thunder, but he could also soar away above the earth as scarcely anyone else could. Listen to a fine performance of his ethereal *Concerto in G Major* if you wish to forget the sorrows of the world. Here is piano music that is transcendental and that carries one along with it. One feels in Beethoven the love of nature. He loved the forest, the brooks, and the peasants, and he put them into his music. He wasn't above a waltz, once in a while, and neither was Schubert, but purely in the spirit of fun.

In Brahms and Schumann we have to master strange rhythms and syncopation, phrases that overlap, that are disturbing at first sight, but come out right in the end, themes that are suddenly changed to half their previous speed—but somehow it all moves on smoothly. Brahms did not compose hastily and his workmanship is most skillful. One needs strong rhythmic feeling and decided heartiness for Brahms; strong accents and broad dynamics, too. His melodies are delightful, but often at first sight of them on the page they seem hidden in a mass of accompanimental material. One must seek them out. Brahms and Schumann are almost the only composers who have made the intermezzo a type of piano piece.

Schumann's style evokes romance above all else. Romance is the mood in the concerto op. 54, in *Carnaval,* in the pieces in op. 12, in *The Forest Scenes,* and even the little romanza in the *Viennese Carnival* op. 26, is a gem in this respect. Much of Schumann's music has a hidden meaning, which must be unearthed before one can thoroughly understand the music. In his letters to Moscheles, Clara Wieck, and others, he explains his meaning and intentions. Show your pupils examples of such things and urge them to study them. Too few pupils have any very definite ideas about them.

NOTES, KEYS, AND TERMS

The French, the Italians, and the Germans express the notes of the scale in terms different from ours. The French and the Italians use the syllables do (ut), re, mi, fa, sol, la, si to correspond to our C,D,E,F,G,A,B. They are based on an ancient Latin hymn, in which each line is sung on the next higher tone until it comes to B, which was arbitrarily called si. The hymn really begins on the syllable "ut," which is still used by the French, although the Italians now use "do" for C.

The initial phrases of each line, the first syllables of which give the notes their names, are as follows:

Ut-queant laxis
Re-sonare fibris
Mi-ra gestorum
Fa-muli tuorum
Sol-ve polluti
La-ii reatum
Sancte Johannes

The names for note duration in England also differ from ours, as follows:

◫ is a breve, or double whole note of eight counts

○ is a semibreve, or whole note

𝅗𝅥 is a minim, or half note

♩ is a crochet, or quarter note

♪ is a quaver, or eighth note

𝅘𝅥𝅯 is a semiquaver, or sixteenth note

𝅘𝅥𝅰 is a demisemiquaver, or thirty-second note

is a hemidemisemiquaver, or sixty-fourth note

84

The names for the key signs in three languages are:

	FRENCH	GERMAN	ITALIAN
the sharp	*dièse*	*Kreuz*	*diesi*
the natural	*bécarre*	*Auflösungs Zeichen*	*biquardo*
the flat	*bémol*	*Versetzungs Zeichen*	*bemolle*

Thus it will readily be seen that in French the key of F sharp is *fa dièse,* and the key of A flat is *la bémol.* In Italian, the key of C sharp is *do diesi,* and the key of E flat is *mi bemolle.*

In French, major is called *majeur:* C major is therefore *ut majeur.* Minor is called *mineur:* A minor is therefore *la mineur.*

In Italian major is *maggiore,* and minor, *minore.*

The Germans have a different way of designating notes and key names, as follows:

C is *Tsay,* but C♯ is *Tsiss,* and C♭, *Tsess*
D is *Day,* but D♯ is *Diss,* and D♭, *Dess*
E is *Ay,* but E♯ is *Ayees,* and E♭, *Ess*
F is *Eff,* but F♯ is *Fiss,* and F♭, *Fess*
G is *Gay,* but G♯ is *Ghiss,* and G♭, *Guess*
A is *Ah,* but A♯ is *Ahees,* and A♭, *Ahss*
B is *Hah,* but B♯ is *Hiss,* and B♭, is *Bay*

It will be seen that according to this notation different words and names may be spelled out, such as BACH, ASCH, SCHEB, and so on, and many composers have written fugues and fantasies on the name of Bach. Schumann used the name of Asch in his *Carnaval* op. 9.

The German word for major is *Dur,* from the Latin *durum,* or hard, thus a piece in E flat major is in *Ess Dur.*

The word for minor in German is *Moll,* which means soft. A piece in F sharp minor is in *Fiss Moll.* Evidently a major key sounds harder on the ear than a minor key.

The effect of crescendo (literally, growing) is expressed in German by the word *zunehmend,* and the opposite effect by the word *abnehmend.*

Italian terms are used almost universally. The reason is simple. The revival of music, after the Middle Ages, began in Italy, and the Italian terms spread to other countries with the spread of Italian music, virtually to become the "music language" of the world. Italian performers and composers carried the language into all countries where music was loved and performed. The meaning and the correct pronunciation of Italian terms should be learned by all pupils, and their teachers are the logical ones to teach them. It is a disgrace to pronounce dolce cantabile, "dols cantabyle," or stringendo with the hard "g" sound. But such pronunciations are often heard, and will continue to be unless corrected. Only a few simple rules are necessary. The vowels are long: A=ah; E=a, as in say; E=e, as in set; I=ee; O=o; U=oo.

The vowels "e" and "i" always soften the consonant before them: Ci=chi; ge=jay; sci=she, as in crescendo; but qui=kwee; and gui=gwee. The ch gives a k sound. In fact, that is the only way to represent it: Schipa=Skeepa; Schichi= Skeekee. The letter "s" at the beginning of a word is ess; but between two vowels it is zee: Caruso=Caruzo. The "gl" is like "ll" in "billiards": Gigli=Jeellyee. The "gn" sounds like "ny": ogni=onyee, really no sound of "g" at all.

THE KEYBOARD STRING INSTRUMENTS

The keyboard as a part of musical instruments extends so far back into the dim past that no one has been able to fix a date for its origin. The hydraulus, the early water organ of Alexandria and Byzantium, certainly had some sort of keys, or knobs, that were used to start the tone; it is highly improbable that they were anything like our keyboards of to-day. It is believed, however, that the keyboard had developed into something like its present form by the early fourteenth century although the earliest clavichord bearing a date was made in Italy in 1537.

At first, the compass was very small, but this was gradually increased. The tone was very weak but very sweet, and it could be varied a trifle after it was produced by moving the key, thereby giving it a slight wave, or vibrato, which was known to the Germans as *Bebung*. This effect of touch was not possible on any of the subsequent instruments. The reason lies in the fact that the tangent, which struck the wire to make the tone, stayed against the wire until the key was released, very much as the finger remains on a violin string for the length of the tone. Thus it allowed the finger to have an intimate connection with the tone. In later instruments, the hammer or plectrum produced the tone and then left the string, so that no such connection was possible.

The action of the clavichord was simplicity itself. A key with a wedge-shaped tangent of brass imbedded in the rear end sprang up and struck the string when the front of the key was depressed, even pressing it upward and changing the pitch a little. The opposite part of the string, beyond that which gave the desired pitch, was stopped by weaving a little strip of cloth or leather between the wires.

Bach, who wrote some of his finest compositions for the clavichord, seems to have loved it more than the harpsichord, or the piano with which he certainly must have been acquainted in his later life. We wonder if he didn't dream of a bigger, stronger tone, more capable of producing the climaxes of the *Chromatic Fantasie and Fugue,* and some of the preludes and fugues in *The Well-Tempered Clavier.* In a room with a seating capacity of four or five hundred people, the tones of the clavichord would be barely audible. It was definitely a house instrument, and was carried from place to place and set up on a table or stool, having no legs of its own.

Next in order came the spinet (in reality, a small harpsichord), the virginal, and the harpsichord. The action in these differed from that of the clavichord in that the tone was produced by picking or plucking the string by a plectrum attached to a jack. At first, a thorn from a bush or tree was used, later, a crow's quill, and ultimately, a little piece of hardened leather, which is the kind of plectrum in use in harpsichords today.

The Latin word for thorn, *spina,* may have been the origin of the name for the spinet, but it is equally likely that it may be traced to an Italian maker named Joannes Spinetus, who worked about 1503.

When the key was struck, a jack, or upright piece, arose. This carried the plectrum, which wedged its way past the string, plucking it. It then sprang back into place, ready for the next time the key was struck. A hog's bristle was used as a spring. Bristles are used for the same purpose in modern harpsichords. The lightninglike rapidity of this action is amazing, and the charm and daintiness of the music of the period can be appreciated only when heard played on the instruments for which it was designed. It seems incredible that so many musicians of fine taste have no interest in "those stupid old instruments of the past." It is almost equivalent to ignoring Bach, Couperin, Rameau, and other early composers. The harpsichord was the usual concert instrument, as its tone was keen and sharp and carried well in a large room. It had several keyboards and sets of strings, and it was equipped with stops to change the effects, which are now controlled by pedals.

There were no pianos earlier than 1709, when Bartolomeo Cristofori, of Florence, began work on four instruments under the patronage of Prince Ferdinand di Medici. He named the new instrument the clavicembalo, which means, literally, a dulcimer with keys. It could be played loud or soft. The name was soon changed to pianoforte, and now we speak simply of the piano. With the pianoforte the instrument had at last arrived in which the control of dynamic effects lay under the player's fingers, instead of in the pedals. One had only to strike the keys with different degrees of strength to get the effect desired.

Cristofori invented hammer action, and it remains much the same today. Naturally, it has been improved upon and finer materials are used, but as a celebrated piano manufacturer has said, "We have never been able to improve on Cristofori's principle." Imagine anyone improving a fine Stradivarius violin! The old craftsmen built better than they knew!

An instrument in which the strings are struck with hammers is always a piano, although many people are deceived by the name "spinet."

The early instruments had no tone-sustaining pedal nor had they much need of one, for their tone was a mere tinkle. The piano that Mozart dragged all over Europe in a carriage had a thin, tinkling tone, and Beethoven's piano was similar. Gradually, a series of improvements added an extra string to each tone, a steel frame, thicker wires, and so on, until the tone reached the magnificent volume and richness that we are familiar with today. It may achieve still greater beauty in years to come by the use of some of the new metals for strings. Who knows?

ON BEING ORIGINAL

To be original perhaps means not so much to discover something entirely new as to discover something by your own mental processes. It may not be entirely new. Is there anything entirely new? Probably not. Every possible interpretation of a Beethoven sonata, for example, has been tried in the past by the army of pianists, and many have proved ineffective. It must appear then that among all these there is one that is the best, and still remains the best. If you try too hard to be original, you may obscure the idea of the composer or the purpose of the composition.

A jerky tempo when the sense of the music is quietness, an overbroad ritardando when it is not in place, a tempo exaggerated in either direction—none of these things indicates a true musician, but rather a musical "tree-sitter," seeking notoriety.

It is often necessary to learn something about what the title of a composition relates to, or the locality of its atmosphere, before discovering its true meaning. Ask your pupils many questions about the composition. Find out what their ideas are. Ask them what the *Kreisleriana* or the *Carnaval* op. 9 means. If they don't know, you must tell them. Be sure that you yourself are informed. Don't try to completely remake a well-known composition. The fake is too obvious. There is music that is so complete and so beautiful that it speaks for itself. All that you need to do is to play it clearly and without exaggeration. Don't try to remake it.

ON GOING ABROAD TO STUDY

Every enthusiastic music student wishes secretly or openly to study in Europe. "Sometime I intend to go abroad to study," has become a commonplace remark. A great deal may be said in favor of it, although it is no longer necessary as far as mere study is concerned. One can get a good musical education today in the institutions and under first-rate teachers in our own country.

Going abroad means a great deal more than that, especially in respect to its broadening and cultural influences, if the student has the right idea. There is also the kind of life in a strange country that, alas, too often turns out altogether wrong. One of the most disheartening sights in large foreign cities is the poor unfortunate student who has quite forgotten why he came. He would much better never have gone.

But there is also the fine opportunity to learn a foreign language, in itself of tremendous cultural value. Strangely enough, many American students ignore this opportunity, and if they learn a few phrases and words by chance, they consider their duty by French and German done.

The opportunity of studying the great architectural monuments, cathedrals, castles, and theaters, of seeing the finest in painting and sculpture, of hearing a great variety of operas, concerts, and recitals, has its rewards. In Paris, recitals usually begin at nine in the evening and frequently later, which makes it rather difficult the next morning. In Germany, they manage this better, concerts and opera beginning at seven o'clock so that one can get home in good time. Here begins a problem that must be solved in some way. Of course, one of the important features of a musical education is to hear and become acquainted with a large mass of music in many forms—operas, symphonies, chamber music recitals, and solo performances. But if one goes out every evening, it definitely encroaches on the energy needed for study during the day. Fortunately, one is not permitted to begin practice before stated hours in the large cities, so that, in a measure, is regulated for the student.

In Paris, in 1929, a fine building designed especially for American students was opened. Known as the American

House, it can house several hundred, with a number of studios for practicing. Its rates are moderate, and its restrictions as to conduct are decent but not severe. Of course, some students prefer to live elsewhere, in a less conformist atmosphere. I believe no other foreign city has gone so far as Paris to provide for American students.

There is always the question of a good teacher, which can be perplexing. Many students start for Europe with no other idea than simply to go there to study. They take up with any teacher, only to become discouraged after a while and ready to throw the whole thing up, and go home.

Have some definite plan before going, and adhere to it. Do not take anyone's word about teachers or you are certain to become confused. Find a good teacher and stay with him until he has a chance to teach you something. No teacher can teach you very much in a week, even if you pay fifty dollars an hour.

Do not be one of those who intentionally take one or two lessons from a famous teacher, just to be able to represent yourself as a pupil of the more famous one. This is quackery and dishonest. You may have been a pupil of the famous teacher, but you surely could not learn much from him in so brief a time.

Berlin, Paris, Vienna, Munich, and Brussels all have magnificent, easily accessible art collections, which offer splendid opportunities for those who enjoy painting and sculpture. These art forms bear such a close analogy to music that it is hard to understand why many music students ignore their existence, and lose such a fine chance for culture. In America, we have less of a chance to see and study fine architecture than in Europe, where nearly every city of importance possesses a fine cathedral or town hall or castle. Get acquainted with them and study them. Goethe said, "Architecture is frozen music." It is profitable to the music student to dissolve and absorb it.

Both Berlin and Paris have two opera houses each, with productions every night during the season, so a large variety of operas may be heard if one has the vitality to take advantage of the opportunity.

Munich, Salzburg, and Bayreuth have summer festivals of opera that are delightful. In many towns there are smaller music festivals that are well worth while, in addition to the pleasure of visiting the delightful cities of Hamburg, Venice, and Heidelberg, to name three where festivals are held. The admission price for concerts and opera is considerably less than in this country. In Brussels, for example, where the Théâtre de la Monnaie gives excellent performances, a good seat can be had for less than a dollar. Altogether, the advantages abroad are very great. On the other hand, some of the best teachers in Europe come to this country and settle here, so one need not feel that it is absolutely necessary to go to Europe to secure a fine musical education. We also have our own fine teachers, who understand the American temperament.

STAGE DEPORTMENT

Suppose you are to give a public performance. Before going out on the stage there are a few things you must remember.

Do not rush out as if you were trying to catch a train.

Do not swing your arms violently.

Walk leisurely to the piano.

If there is applause, wait until you arrive at a spot before the piano before bowing. Some artists try to bow as they walk out on the stage, but it usually gives an impression of awkwardness.

We have seen many kinds of bows. Some artists stand stiffly, and nod the head only slightly. Others bow deeply and often remain too long in that position.

To bow in a manner as simple and as graceful as possible, the body should be inclined from the waist. Smile a little if you like, but don't grin.

Ladies, especially, should stand in front of the piano seat, bow, and then be seated. To approach from behind the seat is awkward, for obvious reasons.

Don't fidget!

If you must use a handkerchief, don't put it on the piano or lay it on the keys. Put it up your sleeve, or on the bench, but *not* on the piano.

Be deliberate about beginning to play. If your heart is fluttering, take a deep breath and close your eyes for a moment. Be sure not to wait too long, or the audience may think you are frightened, which, of course, you are not.

Some fine players have questionable stage manners, and some even strive to be eccentric, but usually bad manners and odd mannerisms detract (and distract) from the music to be played.

Be as easy and as natural as possible.

The day has gone, fortunately, when success depended upon strange antics, long, shaggy manes, and exaggerated movements in playing.

If you are to play a piano accompaniment for some other instrument that has to be tuned, don't sit and thump on A until people in the audience are annoyed. A very soft A can be heard perfectly, and is all that is necessary for the other player to tune by. Remember this and you will present a more musicianly and artistic appearance.

Always settle the tempo in your mind before beginning to play. Many players have wrecked their recitals by starting too fast.

THE FUNDAMENTAL BASS LINE

A very common fault among young pianists, and occasionally among more advanced players, is their neglect of the fundamental line in the bass. Every structure must have something to rest on, and there must be no holes nor weakness in the foundation. It is an excellent plan in lessons to play the bass line straight through the composition. This, of course, does not mean the entire left-hand part, only the bass, to get a good idea of it.

Sometimes the principal melody may be found in the bass. Then it is necessary to exercise care, to shade nicely, as one would with any melody. Many students, in trying to "bring out" a melody, simply play it loud, with very little shading or expression. Remember that a melody may be played piano and still be brought out, as long as the accompaniment is in proper balance. Observe this bass line:

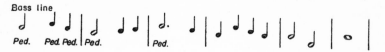

Study the bass line, regardless of the rest of the composition.

NAMES AND WORDS
OFTEN MISPRONOUNCED

Acciaccatura—Short grace note — Ah-chee-ah-cah-*toor*-ah

Aguilar—Spanish lute player — *Ah*-guee-lar
Aïda—Opera by Verdi — Ah-*ee*-dah
Albeniz—Spanish composer — Ahl-*bayn*-yeeth
Appoggiatura—Long grace note — Ah-pog-ja-*too*-rah
Arensky—Russian composer — *Ahr*-en-skee

Bazelaire—French cellist — Baz-*layre*
Berlioz—French composer — Pronounce the z
Boris Godunov— — Bah*rees Go*-doo-nuf
    Opera by Moussorgsky
Borodin—Russian composer — Bo-*rud*-dyn
Borowski—Anglo-Polish composer — Bo-*ruf*-skee
Busoni—Italian Pianist — Boo-*zone*-ee
Busser—French composer-organist — Beu-*sayr*

Caruso—Opera tenor — Cah-*roo*-zo
Casadesus—French pianist — Kass-ahd-*su*
Cassado—Spanish cellist — Cassah-*do*
Cavalleria Rusticana— — Cah-val-er-*ee*-ah
    Opera by Mascagni — Roos-tee-*cah*-nah
                    Mahs-*cahn*-yee

Cembalo—Musical instrument — *Chem*-bah-lo
Chaliapin—Russian basso profundo — Shah-lee-*ah*-peen
Charpentier—French composer — Shar-pont-*yay*
Claessens—Opera singer — *Clah*-sens

Dallier—French organist — Dahl-*yay*
Dargomijsky— — Dahr-*gom*-ish-kee
    Russian composer-pianist
Delmas—French opera baritone — Pronounce the s
Dobrzynski—Polish pianist-composer — Dobr-*zjin*-skee
Dóhnanyi— — *Doh*-nan-yee
    Hungarian composer-pianist

Drdla—Czech composer

Drrrrdla (trill the r strongly)

Dukas—French composer

Pronounce the s

Dvořák—Czech composer

Dvor-shahk (trill the r)

Erlanger—French composer

Air-long-*jay*

Eugen Onegin—
      Opera by Tchaikovsky

On-*yay*-ghin

Euryanthe—Opera by Weber

Oyre-*an*-tay

Fair at Sorotschinsk, The—
      Opera by Moussorgsky

Sor-*otch*-insk

Figaro—Character in *The Barber
      of Seville* and *The Marriage
      of Figaro*

Feé-gar-o

Forza del Destino—Opera by Verdi

Fortsa del Des-*tee*-no

Gade—Danish composer

Gah-thah

Garbusova—Russian cellist

Gar-*boo*-so-vah

Gatti-Casazza—Opera impresario

Gah-tee-caz-*zat*-za

Gevaert—Flemish composer

Gay-*vahrt*

Gianni Schichi—Opera by Puccini

Jan-ee *Skee*-kee

Gioconda, La—Opera by
      Ponchielli

Jo-*kon*-da
Pon-kee-*a*-lee

Giordano—Italian composer

Jor-*dah*-no

Glazounov—Russian composer

Glah-zoo-noff

Godowski—Polish pianist

Go-*duff*-skee

Götterdämmerung—Opera by Wagner

Accent first syllable.

Gretchanínov—Russian composer

Gretch-*an*-ínoff

Grovlez—French composer

Gro-vlay

Guglielmi—Italian composer

Gool-*yel*-mee

Habanera—Spanish dance

Ah-van-*air*-ah

Hänsel und Gretel—
      Opera by Humperdinck

Hen-sel und *Gray*-tel

Hérodiade—Opera by Massenet

Air-o-dee-*ad*

Honegger—Swiss composer

O-ne-*gher*

Hopak—Russian dance

Go-pak

Horowitz—Russian pianist

Gor-o-witz

Hüe, Georges—French composer

Uee

Iturbi—Spanish pianist   Ee-*toor*-be

Janáček—Czech composer   *Yahn*-a-shek
Jommelli—Italian singer-composer   Yo-*mell*-ee
Juive, La—Opera by Halévy   Zhoo-*eev*

Karsavina—Russian dancer   Kahr-*sav*-ee-nah
Khovantchina—   Kho-*vahn*-chee-nah
    Opera by Moussorgsky
Kodaly—Hungarian composer   *Ko*-dahe

L'Africaine—Opera by Meyerbeer   Laf-ree-*cane*
Lakmé—Opera by Delibes   Lack-*may*
Lalo—French composer   Lah-*low*
Lucia di Lammermoor—   Loo-*chee*-ah
    Opera by Donizetti

Maelzel—Inventor of the Metronome *Male*-tzel
Maeterlinck—Belgian poet-dramatist *Mah*-ter-link
Mandragora—Song   Mahn-*drah*-gorah
Manon Lescaut—Opera by Puccini Les-*ko*
Messerer—French composer   Mess-air-*rair*
Mignon—Opera by Thomas   Meen-*yon* (To-*mah*)

Nordraak—Norwegian composer   *Noor*-droke

Pagliacci, Il—Opera by Leoncavallo   Pah-lyee-*ah*-chee
Paisiello—Italian composer   Pahee-se-*ay*-lo
Paladilhe—French composer   Pah-lah-*deel*
Pick-Mangiagalli—Italian composer Peek-Manja-*gah*-lee
Pique Dame, La—   Peek Dam
    Opera by Tchaikovsky
Pohjola's Daughter—   *Poh*-yoh-lah
    Symphonic fantasy by Sibelius
Ponchielli—Italian composer   Pon-kee-*ay*-lee
Pons—French soprano   Pongs
Porpora—Italian composer   *Por*-por-ah

Rabaud—French composer-conductor Rah-*bo*
Rachmaninoff—   Rach-*mahn*-e-noff
    Russian pianist-composer

Remenyi—Hungarian violinist	*Rem*-en-yee
Roi d'Ys, Le—Opera by Lalo	Rwah-dees
Rotoli—Italian-American singer-composer	*Ro*-to-lee
Saint-Saëns—French composer	San-son(g)s
Samároff—American pianist	Sah-*mah*-roff
Santoliquido—Italian composer	Sahnto-*lig*-ui-do
Schalchi—Italian singer	*Skahl*-kee
Shostakovich—Russian composer	Shos-tah-*ko*-vich
Snegourotschka— Opera by Rimski-Korsakov	*Snyay*-goo-rotch-kah
Swan of Tuonela, The— Tone poem by Sibelius	Doo-*on*-a-lah
Sźigeti—Hungarian violinist	Accent first syllable
Thaïs—Opera by Massenet	Tah-*ees* (Mass-*nay*)
Trovatore, Il—Opera by Verdi	Tro-vah-*to*-ray
Walhall—Hall of the Slain	*Vahl*-hahl
Walküre, Die—Opera by Wagner	*Vahl*-kure
Zandonai—Italian composer	*Tzahn*-don-ay

TERMS AND QUESTIONS
FOR EXAMINATIONS

For First Year Students

meno—less
più—more
molto, assai—very
poco—little
poco a poco—little by little
con—with
senza—without
leggiero—lightly
pesante—heavily
diminuendo—diminishing in tone
crescendo—increasing in tone
agitato—agitated
sostenuto—sustained
tranquillo—quietly
l'istesso—the same
l'istesso tempo—the same tempo
simile, seque—continuing in like manner
rallentando, ritardando—growing slower
ritenuto—in slower time
ando, endo—*ing* suffixes
uto, ato—*ed* suffixes
accelerándo, affretándo, stringéndo—hurrying
incalzándo, strétto—hurrying
etto, ino—diminutive endings
mancándo—lacking in speed
perdéndosi—losing itself
smorzándo—extinguishing
calándo—softer and slower
slentándo—becoming slower
stentándo—dragging
moréndo—dying away
sforzando—strongly accented
slargando, allargando—broadening in effect
più mosso, più moto—more motion, faster

meno mosso—less motion, slower
allegro—fast
allegretto—a little slower
largo—slow
larghetto—a little slow, not as slow as largo.
andante—going
andantino—going a little

1. Explain the different ways of making a note important: striking it louder, pausing before it, holding it longer.
2. What is meant by rubato?
3. What is ensemble music?
4. What is chamber music? Why so called?
5. Explain dynamics.
6. Explain syncopation.
7. What is the difference between "emotional" and "intellectual" piano playing?
8. What instruments besides the piano are used in a conventional piano trio? (usually violin and cello) A piano quartet? (violin, viola, and cello) A piano quintet? (String quartet)
9. What is a concerto?
10. From what instrument is the piano derived?
11. What do you consider the greatest assets in teaching the piano? (development of finger and wrist independence, sense of rhythm, playing of compound rhythms three against two, three against four, etc., good position, memorizing)

For Second Year Students

più tosto—more nearly
piacevole—pleasantly, free from strong accents
a piacére, ad líbitum—at the pleasure of the player
maestóso—majestically
allegro maestóso—slower than ordinary allegro
grazióso—gracefully
giústo—strict, opposed to rubato
giocóso—jokingly
giojóso—joyously

gigue, giga—jig (An old instrument preceding the violin, but something like it. A piece played on it.)

cedez—ritardando

suivez—follow (literally, to follow the solo part in a ritardando)

velóce, volante, sciolto, agilita—rapidly

strepitóso (con strepito)—furiously, noisily

lusingándo—caressingly

1. What makes a chord major or minor? What interval?
2. Explain dotted notes.
3. Double dotted notes.
4. In playing a D.C. or D.S. passage, are the first repeats observed?
5. Give the words for which D.C. stands. For D.S.
6. Explain the signs for right and left hands in French and Italian. *(Right:* Fr., main droite, M.D.; It., mano destro, M.D. *Left:* Fr., main gauche, M.G., It., mano sinistra, M.S.)
7. Explain grace notes. The different kinds. How they are played. How the short grace note is written. What they indicate when written before a trill.
8. What are arpeggiated chords? The long lines; the short lines? From what is "arpeggio" derived? (arpa—harp)
9. Explain holds. How long. Approaching a hold. After a hold.
10. Explain 8va lines over a passage. Under a passage in the bass. Loco. Under a bass note.
11. What is an enharmonic change? (A change of notation without a change of pitch)
12. Explain how one plays expressively (espressivo). Should everything be played expressively? A scherzo? Marziale? Allegro giusto? Are most slow movements in the expressive style?
13. What is meant by an accidental?

For Third Year Students

mesto, dolente, con dolore—sadly

bis—twice, repeat

mezzo forte—half loud
mezzo piano—half soft
sopra—over, above (refers to crossing hands)
sotto—under
doppio—double
doppio movimento—twice as fast
ben misurato—well in time
lunga pausa—long pause
berceuse, Wiegenlied—cradle song
martellato—hammered, clangorous
marziale—martial, march time
con tutta la forza—with all the force (full strength)
con fuoco—with fire, energy
con brio—with elegance, brilliantly
con bravura—dashingly (literally, with bravery)
scherzando—playfully
con anima—with soul
appassionato—passionately, with strong feeling

1. What is a cadenza? In what movements of a concerto do cadenzas usually occur? In earlier times how was the cadenza played?
2. Explain an organ or pedal point. Is is always found in the same voice?
3. Explain passing notes.
4. What is meant by phrasing? What is probably the earliest origin of phrasing?
5. What is meant by turns? How many tones are comprised? By mordents? How many tones? By a downward stroke through the mordent? By an accidental above or below a mordent or turn?
6. Explain the following abbreviations: mf, mp, mv, pf, p, pp, f, ff.
7. Does an accidental on a degree on either staff necessarily affect the same degree on the other staff?
8. What is common time? How indicated? A stroke through the C means what? Where does the accent come?
9. How many beats in a measure of 6-8 time? Where is the strong accent? How many beats in a measure of 6-4 time? Of 9-8 time? Of 12-8 time? What one single note will fill a measure of 12-8 time?

For Fourth Year Students

glissando—sliding
disinvolto—free and easy, gracefully
alla breve—4-4 time played in two beats
cantábile, cantando—in a singing style
ben cantando—well sung, a very singing tone (not necessarily loud)
commodo—easy, comfortable
allegro commodo—comfortably fast
una corda—left pedal to be used (one string, literally)
tre corde—release the left pedal (three strings, literally)
intermezzo—an interlude
obbligato—required, indispensible
rinforzando—reinforcing
stridente—noisy, harsh
tenuto—held full length
subito—quickly, at once (at the end of a page, it means turn quickly)

1. Give the equivalent of a measure of 6-8 time in one note. Also a rest. Can you do the same in a measure of 9-8?
2. Who invented the scale fingering we use today?
3. When did the thumb come into use in playing piano? Who began the use of the thumb on the black keys?
4. Who began the practice of giving piano recitals from memory?
5. Explain the different touches: legato, staccato, demi-staccato, portamento.
6. What is an ictus? An anacrusis? Give examples.
7. What is a masculine ending? A feminine ending?
8. Explain metronome marks. M.M. ♩=42. ♩=96. ♩.=♩
9. Explain the use of pedals. Give the meaning of una corda; of tre corde. How does the soft pedal work on a grand piano? On an upright piano? The damper pedal? What is the middle pedal on a grand piano?
10. Give the names of some Americans who have become famous in opera. (Examples: Nordica, Homer, Farrar, Whitehill, Martin, Althouse, Tibbett, Traubel, Risé Stevens.) Some American pianists. (Examples: Sherwood,

Samároff, Cottlow, Bloomfield, Schelling.) Some American violinists. (Examples: M. Powell, A. Spalding, Macmillen, Eddy Brown, Max Rosen, Helen Ware.) Some American composers. (Examples: H. W. Parker, MacDowell, G. Chadwick, J. A. Carpenter.)

SUGGESTED TOPICS FOR A PAPER

1. *Expression.* Dynamic expression. Espressivo. What it means. How obtained.
2. *Memorizing.* Importance of, and ways of, memorizing. When to begin. Testing the memory.
3. *Mannerisms.* Enumerate. Why they are objectionable.
4. *Phrasing.* Earliest origin. Meaning. Different kinds. How accomplished. When to employ it.
5. *Touches.* Cultivation. Importance. Different kinds. Describe clearly.
6. *Right kind of practicing.* As distinct from practice by the clock.
7. *Sight reading.* How to improve it. Its importance. What not to do in the beginning. What to do.
8. *Interpretation.* What it is. Models. Standards. Exaggerations. Difficulty.
9. *Melody playing.* What to avoid. Advantages of listening. Avoid flat melodies. Accompaniment. Agreement with the melody. Dynamic grade.
10. *Nervousness.* In public performance. Varieties. Causes. Possible remedies.
11. *Estimating a pupil's needs.* At first hearing. Things to observe.
12. *The lazy pupil.*
13. *The overconfident pupil.*
14. *The timid pupil.*
15. *The expressionless pupil.*
16. *Dynamics.* Meaning. Some misapprehensions. Terms indicating dynamic changes.
17. *Agogics.* Meaning. Employment.
18. *Daily setting-up exercises.* Importance.
19. *The ritardando.* Equivalents in other languages. Sostenuto. What is a good ritardando. Poor. Ritenuto. Other words of similar meaning.
20. *The hold.* Other names for it. Preparation. How long after the pause mark.
21. *The mordent.* Different kinds. Derivation of the name. How it is played.

22. *The turn.* Kinds. Execution. What governs it.
23. *The trill.* How best to study it to acquire proficiency.
24. *Embellishments.* Care in use. Dynamic importance.
25. *Program building.* Different kinds of programs. Dangers. What to avoid.
26. *Fingering.* Good and bad.
27. *Chords.* Touch. Practice. Notes to be brought out. Studies.
28. *Rhythm.* Its importance. Varieties of rhythmic patterns. Meter.
29. *The thumb.* Training. Stiff thumb.
30. *The pedals.* Uses of each. How to acquire. Effects.
31. *The choice of material for the pupils.* Variety. Usefulness.
32. *Highly specialized taste in music.* Dangers.
33. *Good taste.* How to acquire. Models. Traditions.
34. *Determining the correct tempo.* Dangers.
35. *Assignment of work.* Making clear what to study.
36. *Division of practice.* In accordance with amount of time available.
37. *Criticism of the pupil.* How to encourage it. How to correct it. Tact.
38. *Octaves.* Their indispensability. Different kinds of octaves.
39. *Inflections.* Accents. Cadences.
40. *General style and finish.* When notes, time, and tempo are all there and still something is greatly lacking, what to look for.
41. *Tempo rubato.* Describe. Dangers.
42. *Being original.* Conception of the term. Pitfalls.
43. *Relaxation.* Importance. Dangers.
44. *Imagination in playing.* Importance of having a mental image to project.

APPENDIX

NOTE

The following lists comprise (1) an unusully wide selection of piano exercises, studies, and compositions suitable for pupils from Grade 3 through Grade 7; (2) an even more comprehensive selection of compositions for the piano alone and in combination with a variety of other instruments; and (3) a brief bibliography of books on musical subjects, biographies of musicians, and works of fiction and semifiction with a music background, all of which should hold some interest for the serious student of the piano.

After some of the titles of the piano literature, comments regarding their special suitability have been parenthetically added.

GRADE 3
EXERCISES AND STUDIES FOR TECHNIQUE

Berens, H.—Op. 70. *50 Easy Studies without Octaves* (Presser)
———— Op. 79. *20 Studies without Octaves*
Bertini—Op. 100. *25 Progressive Studies without Octaves*
Czerny—Op. 139. *100 Progressive Studies without Octaves*
Döring, C. H.—Op. 86. *16 Easy Melodious Studies*
Duvernoy—Op. 176. *25 Studies*
Gurlitt—Op. 82. *First Steps for the Young Player* (Schirmer Library, No. 534)
———— Op. 90. *50 Daily Exercises in Canon Form* (Schirmer Library, No. 834)
———— Op. 117. *First Lessons* (Schirmer Library, No. 324)
———— Op. 141. *Velocity for Beginners*
Hunten—Op. 38. *Melodious Studies*
Köhler—Op. 151. *Very Easy Studies*
————Op. 157. *Somewhat More Advanced*
———— Op. 232. *First Lessons in Finger Dexterity*
Le Couppey—Op. 17. *The Alphabet*
Lemoine—Op. 37
Loeschhorn—Op. 84. *3 Books*

———— Op. 65. *Melodious Studies*
Streabog—Op. 63. *12 Melodious Studies*
Terry, Frances—Op. 101. *Melodious Pieces* (Etudes Miniatures)

SONATINAS, ETC.

Bach—*Little Preludes*
Bach-Carroll—*First Lessons in Bach* (Schirmer Library, No. 1436)
Bach-MacDowell—*Six Little Pieces*
Beethoven—*Sonatina in F Major*
Clementi—Op. 36, Nos. 1, 2 and 3. (progressive)
Czerny—Op. 706, No. 1.
Janke, G.—Op. 19, No. 1. *Sonatine in C*
Kuhlau—Op. 20. Sonatinas Nos. 1, 2 and 3
Lange—Op. 78. Sonatinas 1 to 4.
Lichner—Op. 4. *Sonatina*
———— Op. 49. Sonatinas 1, 2 and 3.
———— Op. 31, No. 1. *Polonaise*
Reinecke—Op. 98, Nos. 8 and 9.
Sartorio—Op. 368. *12 Instructive Pieces*
Schumann—Op. 68, No. 4. *Choral*

PIECES IN MORE ENTERTAINING STYLE

Bachmann—*Gavotte Duchesse*
Bertini—Op. 166. *12 Little Pieces and Preludes*
Engel, S. C.—Op. 31, No. 3. *The Juggler* (scales, etc.)
————Op. 31, No. 4. *Polonaise in D*
————Op. 31, No. 7. *Hungarian Dance in E* (rhythms)
Handel—*Seven Pieces*
———— *Six Fugues*
Hummel—Op. 11. *Rondo in E Flat*
Klengel—*Canons and Fugues* (2 Books)
Kuhlau—Op. 55. Sonatas 1 to 6
———— Op. 59. Sonatas 1 to 3
———— Op. 66. *3 Sonatinas*
———— Op. 88. *4 Sonatinas*
Mendelssohn—Op. 72. *Kinderstücke*
Merkel—Op. 173. *2 Sonatinas in G and F*
Mozart—*Sonata No. 1 in C Major*
———— *Sonata No. 2 in G Major*

Mozart-Bendel—*Adagio Favori*
Reinecke—*Toccatina*
———— *Variations on a Theme by Handel*
Rheinberger—*Toccatina*
Rheinhold—Op. 45. *Suite*
Rosenhain—*Andante and Rondo*

PIECES, ETC.

Bach—*Little Prelude in D*
————*Prelude and Fugue in F* (difficulties evenly distributed)
Beethoven—*6 Variations on Original Theme in G*
Döring—Op. 8, No. 11. *Prelude*
————*Wave Whispers* (melody in top line of triplet accompaniment)
Elmenreich—Op. 14, No. 4. *Spinning Song*
Emery, Stephen—Op. 13, No. 11. *Under the Pines* (D flat)
———— Op. 18, No. 2. *Fingertwist*
———— Op. 13, No. 12. *Wellenspiel*
Friml, R.—Op. 80, Nos. 1 to 5. *Pastoral Scenes*
Gade, N.—Op. 36, Nos. 1 to 5. *Christmas Pieces*
Gounod—*Les Pifferari in F*
Groton, F.—*Moods and Motions*
Handel—*Bourrée in G Major*
Hause, Carl—Op. 102. *Staccato Etude* (a few octaves)
Heller—Op. 46. *Study* (running work in 16ths)
———— Op. 46, No. 5. *Velocity Study*
Henselt—Op. 5. *Love Song* (melody in the tenor, carried by the thumbs)
Janke—Op. 11. *Etude* (energetic, rhythmic; valuable study)
Jensen, A.—Op. 33, No. 5. *Elfin Dance* (scherzo style, must go fast)
Jensen, G.—*Elfentanz*
Kirchner—Op. 71. *On the Village Green* (legato finger action —16th notes)
Klein, B. O.—*Skating*
———— Op. 43, No. 2. *Märchen*
———— Op. 43, No. 8. *Abendlied*
Köhler—Op. 210. *Little Cradle Song*
Krause—Op. 2, No. 2. *Etude* (triplet figures)
Kronke, E.—Op. 110. (in ballade style, trifling)

Kullak, T.—*Scenes from Childhood.* (12 numbers)
Lemont, Cedric—*Six Melodic Studies*
Loeschhorn—Op. 96. *Aus der Kinderwelt* (two books)
———— Op. 100. *Aus der Kinderwelt* (two books)
Mathews—*Standard Grade Course, Book IV*
Mayer, Charles—*Romance Italienne*
———— Op. 340, Book I. *Little Pieces*
Mozart—*Minuet No. 1*
Nollet—*Tempo Guisto* (rapid sextolet figures in right hand,
        some octaves)
Pierné—*Petite Gavotte in G Major*
Ravina—*Etude for Style in C Major* (right-hand work)
Rheinhold—Op. 52, No. 2. *Am Springbrunnen*
———— Op. 39, No. 1. *March of Fingal's Men*
———— Op. 39, No. 4. *Waltz*
Rudorff—Op. 10, No. 1. *Fantasiestücke*
Schumann—*Album for the Young* (selections)
Schytte—Op. 58. *Etude* (rapid triplets)
———— Op. 66. *Witches' Dance*
Spindler—Op. 123. *The Gazelle* (right-hand finger work)
Von Wilm, N.—Op. 8, No. 1. *Berceuse*
———— Op. 12. *2 Books of Easy Pieces*
———— Op. 24. *Peasant Dance*
Wachs—*A mon Moulin*
Weiss—*Spinning Wheel*
———— Op. 5. *Rondino*
Wolff, B.—*Happy Home Coming*

GRADE 4
ETUDES AND TECHNICAL STUDIES

Burgmüller—Op. 109. *18 Characteristic Studies*
Concone—Op. 24. *25 Studies*
———— Op. 30. *25 Studies for Singing Tone*
Cooke, J. F.—*Mastering Scales and Arpeggios*
Cross, M.—Book 2. *Daily Exercises for Both Hands*
———— Books 2 and 3. *Standard Exercises for Left Hand*
Czerny—Op. 261. *101 Passages*
———— Op. 636. *Preliminary to School of Dexterity*
———— Op. 718. (3 books, especially for the left hand)

Döring—Op. 39. (3 books)
——— Op. 8. (3 books)
——— Op. 38. (3 books)
Duvernoy—Op. 120. (3 books)
Gurlitt—Op. 80. *Rhythmical Studies* (3 books)
——— Op. 90. *50 Canonic Studies*
Hassert—Op. 50. *Velocity* (various styles)
Heller—Op. 47. (slightly easier than op. 45, style)
——— Op. 45.
——— Op. 125. *24 Etudes in Expression*
Heller-Philipp—*Studies in Musicianship*
Köhler—Op. 234. *24 Musical Studies*
——— 239. *14 Rhythmical Studies* (2 books)
Krause—Op. 2. *Trill Studies*
——— Op. 12. *10 Left Hand Studies*
Kunz—*200 Little Canons*
Renaud—Op. 145. *20 Studies* (Books I and II, entertaining style)
Riemann—*Studies in Polyphonic Playing*
Rogers, J. H.—Op. 40. (2 books)
Smith, W. G.—*8 Measure Studies for Daily Practice* (2 books)
Terry, Frances—*Etudes Miniatures*

SONATAS, ETC.

Bach, C. P. E.—*Allegro*
——— *Solfeggietto*
Bach, J. S.—*First Lessons in Book II* (by Walter Carroll)
——— *Bourrées in A and A Minor*
——— *Two Voiced Inventions*
——— *Prelude and Fugue in C. No. 1*
Beethoven—*Six Variations on "Nel Cor Piu"* (Paganini)
——— *Sonatina in G Minor*
Clementi—Op. 26. *Sonata in D Major*
——— Op. 36, Nos. 5 and 6.
——— *Toccata in B Flat*
Field—*Rondo in E Flat*
Haydn—*Sonata No. 1 in G* (turns)
——— *Sonata No. 3 in F*
——— *Gipsy Rondo*

———— *Rondo in A*

———— *Sonata in E Flat Major, No. 17* (Haydn's biggest sonata)

———— *Fantasie in C Major* (this and the following *Variations* are contained in No. 484, Peters edition.)

———— *Variations in F Minor* (difficult for most players.)

Mozart—*Sonata in A Major* (begins with a theme and variations)

———— *Sonata in D Major, No. 13* (spirited, good rondo for technic)

———— *Sonata in F, No. 4*

———— *Sonata in A Minor* (said to show the influence of Handel)

Schumann—Op. 118. *Sonata No. 3 in C Major*

PIECES

Borodin—*Serenade in B Flat*

Brassin—Op. 17. *Nocturne* (middle part a sort of spinning song effect)

Chaminade—Op. 39. *Toccata in C Minor* (velocity and style)

———— Op. 24. *Les Libellules*

D'Albert—*Melody*

Durand—Op. 62. *Chaconne*

Duvernoy—Op. 206. *Feu Roulant*

Gade—Op. 41. *Im Walde* (rustling of the forest, horn sounds)

Godard—Op. 14. *The Swallows, En Courant, Guirlandes,* and *Venetienne*

———— Op. 16. *Gavotte in B*

Grieg—*Berceuse in G*

———— Op. 6. *Humoresques, I - IV*

GRADE 5
ETUDES

Augieras—*25 Studies for the Left Hand* (Schirmer)

Berens—Op. 61. *School of Velocity* (4 vols., Universal)

Burgmüller—Op. 89. *Left Hand Studies* (Universal)

———— Op. 105. *12 Brilliant Studies*

Clementi—*Preludes and Exercises* (Universal)

Czerny—Op. 337. *40 Daily Studies in Every Style* (Peters. Indispensable)

———— Op. 718. *Left Hand Studies*

———— Op. 299. *Velocity Studies* (books 1, 2, 3 and 4)

Doenhoff—*6 Advanced Studies for Small Hands*

———— *3 Modern Piano Etudes*

Döring—Op. 39. *Studies* (3 books)

Heller—Op. 16. *Art of Phrasing* (2 books, progressive)

Jensen—Op. 32. *Etudes for Style and Expression.* (3 books, unexcelled)

Köhler—Op. 135. *15 Brilliant Studies*

Krinke—*Exercises for Extension and Muscular Control* (Schirmer)

Kronke—Op. 129. *Advanced Rhythmic Studies* (excellent) (Schirmer)

Le Couppey—Op. 25. *La Difficulte* (mostly for right hand)

Loeschhorn—Op. 66 (books 1, 2 and 3)

Poldini—Op. 96. *Poetic Studies*

Reinhardt—*Exercises for the Development of the Fourth and Fifth Fingers* (Schirmer)

Schmidt—Op. 16. *Studies in Various Styles*

SONATAS, PRELUDES, ETC.

Bach, J. S.—2 bourrées from *Suite 1* (Church edition of suites, A major and A minor)

———— *Three voiced Inventions*

———— *The Well Tempered Clavier,* Book 2. (preludes and fugues)

Bach-Friedmann—*Allegro*

Beethoven—Op. 2, No. 1. *Adagio* (an excellent study, employing all kinds of turns, three notes against four, two notes against three, etc.)

———— *Andante in F* (requires good octave technic)

———— *Rondo in G Major*

———— *Rondo in C Major*

———— *Variations in F*

———— Op. 129. *Rondo a Capriccio*

———— Op. 26. *Sonata*

———— Op. 2, No. 2. *Sonata*

Grieg—Op. 43. *Butterfly* (very difficult in a certain way)
———— Op. 43. *An den Frühling*
———— Op. 54. *Nocturne in C Major* (poetic, difficult rhythms)
Grutzmacher—Op. 66. *Albumleaf* (arpeggios between the hands)
———— *Melody*
Handel—*Variations in E* (commonly called "The Harmonious Blacksmith" in English)
———— *Lessons, Chaconne, Fugues* (Peters ed., No. 4)
Haydn—*Adagio in E Major* (excellent for interpretation and style.) (Peters)
———— *Sonata in D Major* (short largo; good rondo for speed)
———— *Sonata in F Major*
———— *Sonata in E Minor*
———— *Sonata in C Sharp Minor, No. 8* (difficult key, rhythmic problems)
———— *Sonata in E Flat Major, No. 14*
Heller—Op. 151. *2 Etudes* (light velocity in the right hand)
Korngold—Op. 3, No. 4. *Wichtelmännlein*
Philipp—*The Elf*
Rheinberger—*The Chase* (interesting rhythmically)
———— Op. 7. *Ballade in G Minor* (every pianist should play it)
———— *Fugue in G Minor*
Schütt—*Etude Mignonne*
———— Op. 20, No. 3. *Scherzino* (excellent study, canonic, expressive) (Schirmer)
———— Op. 20, No. 5. *Arabesque*
Russian Song (transcription) (Schirmer)
Weber, Gustav—Op. 7, No. 2. *Butterflies* (Schirmer)

GRADE 6
ETUDES

Clementi—*Gradus ad Parnassum* (Good left-hand studies)
Cramer—*Selected Studies*
Czerny—Op. 399, Books I-II. (left hand)
———— Op. 740. *Finger Dexterity*
———— Op. 755. *Perfection in Style* (legato, octaves, etc.)

———— Op. 261. *Passage Playing*

———— Op. 365. *Virtuosity*

———— Op. 337. *Daily Exercises*

Kessler—*Chords* (No. 13 in *Nouveau Gradus ad Parnassum,* by Philipp.) (Leduc ed.)

Mayer—*Lightness* (No. 20, in above)

Moscheles—Op. 70, Books I-II.

Moscheles-Joseffy—*First Etude* (remarkable study for fingers) (Schirmer)

Philipp—*La Vélocité* (2 books, all kinds of problems) (Leduc)

———— *The Czerny Technique* (universal exercises) (Heugel)

———— *15 Studies by Clementi, Czerny, Chopin, Cramer, etc.* (Heugel)

———— *Finger Independence* (daily studies)

———— *Exercises de tenues* (daily studies)

Schneider, Robert—Op. 11. *Spannungsetuden* (for stretching tight and small hands) (Boosey and Hawkes)

Thalberg—Op. 26, No. 1. *The Trill* (in Philipp's *Nouveau Gradus*)

SONATAS, TOCCATAS, ETC.

Bach, J. S.—*English Suite No. 4*

———— *Fantasie in C Minor*

———— *Partita No. 1 in B Flat* (arr. by Harold Bauer)

———— *Partita No. 5 in G*

———— (*Toccata in G*) (arr. by Harold Bauer)

———— *The Well Tempered Clavier* (preludes and fugues)

Bauer, Harold—*Great Composers of the Past*

Beethoven—*Sonata,* op. 13 (Pathétique)

———— *Sonata,* op. 26 (especially the rondo)

———— *Sonata,* op. 7

———— *Sonata,* op. 10, I, II and III

———— *Sonata,* op. 14, No. 1

———— *Rondo,* op. 129

D'Albert—*Suite,* op. 1

Freyer, Herbert—*Six Little Variations on a Rigadoon by Purcell* (Schott)

Gollnelli—Op. 145. *Toccata No. 29* (in Philipp's *Nouveau Gradus*)

Handel—*Transcriptions* (by William Murdoch): *Prelude and Allegro, Sonata in A Minor, Andante and Allegro* (Schott)

———— *Suites* I-VIII (Peters)

Handel-Von Buelow—*Gigue in G Minor*

Handel-Whiting—*Suite in G* (Schirmer)

Henius, Joseph—*Early Piano Transcriptions* (Paradisi, Turini, Couperin, Kirnberger) (Carl Fischer)

Lachner, V.—Op. 157. *Prelude and Toccata*

Martini, Padre—*Prelude and Fugue in E Minor* (*Early Italian Music,* by Esposito) (Ditson)

Mendelssohn—Op. 54. *Variations Sérieuses*

———— Op. 104. 3 *Preludes* (light finger action)

———— *Prelude and Fugue in E Minor*

———— Op. 35. *Prelude and Fugue in E Minor*

Moszkowski—*Advanced Studies in Double Notes* Book IV. (Enoch and Sons)

Mozart—*Sonata No.* 13, *D Major*

———— *Sonata No* 15, *D Major*

———— *Sonata No.* 9, *A Major*

———— *Sonata No.* 14, *D Major*

———— *Sonata No.* 17, *C Major*

Pierné, G.—Op. 40. *Prelude and Fuguetta* (Hamelle)

Raff—Op. 204. *Suite*: (*Prelude, Sarabande, Rigadon and Tamborin*)

Rameau—*The Three Hands* (MacDowell) (Schmidt)

Rheinberger—Op. 7. *Ballade in G Minor*

———— Op. 12. *Toccata*

Scarlatti—*The Cat's Fugue*

Scarlatti-Tausig—*Sonata in C Major* (Schott)

Weber—Op. 49. Rondo from 3rd Sonata

Weber-Tchaikovsky—*Perpetual Movement* (arr. for left hand)

CONCERT PIECES

Chaminade—*Le Retour* (Church)

———— *Autumn*

———— *Les Libellules*

Cui, C.—Op. 40, No. 6. *Causerie* (Schirmer)

Fauré, G.—Op. 33, No. 1. *Nocturne in E Flat*

—————— Op. 33. No. 2. *Nocturne in A Flat*
Godard—*Le Chevalier Fantastique*
—————— *Mignon*
—————— *Pan*
Grieg—Op. 41. (3 of his own songs arr. by himself for piano: *Cradle Song, Klein Haakon, Ich Liebe Dich*)
—————— Op. 19. *Norwegian Bridal Procession: On the Mountains, Carnaval*
Gernsheim—Op. 59, Book 2, No. 5. *Eolus* (Rieter-Biedermann)
Glazounov—Op. 49. *Gavotte in D*
—————— *La Nuit* (etude)
Jensen—Op. 42. *Canzonetta*
—————— Op. 44. *Erotikon*
—————— Op. 43. *Dryade* (difficult left hand)
Leschetizky—Op. 40, No. 6. *Consolation*
Liadov—*Barcarolle*
Liszt—*Consolation in D Flat*
—————— *Valse Impromptu in A Flat*
—————— *Gondoliera*
—————— *Valse Oubliée*
—————— *Liebestraum*
—————— *Sonnetta di Petrarca, No. 123*

GRADE 7
STUDIES

Brahms—*51 Technical Studies*
Czerny—Op. 802. (2 books of scales in thirds, etc.)
Kessler, J. C.—Op. 20. (2 books)
Philipp—*New Gradus ad Parnassum* (a vast collection of studies for various purposes by many different composers, some of them for recital programs)
Tausig—*Daily Studies*

CONCERT PIECES

Alabieff-Liszt—*The Nightingale*
Alkan—*Le Vent* (concert etude)
Arensky—Op. 43. *6 Caprices*

———— *Basso Ostinato*
———— Op. 20. *Bigarrures*
———— *Scherzo*
———— Op. 36. *Etude in F Sharp Major*
Bach-Busoni—*Prelude and Fugue in D Major*
Bach-D'Albert—*Prelude and Fugue in D Major*
———— *Prelude and Fugue on the Name of B-A-C-H*
Bach-Joseffy—*Prelude, Air and Bourrée*
Bach-Liszt—*Organ Prelude and Fugue in A Minor*
Bach-Mannes—*Prelude from Violin Sonata* (Ditson)
Bach-Philipp—*Choral Preludes*
Bach-Reger—*Prelude and Fugue in D Major*
Bach-Rummel—*Cembalo Obbligato.* Series III (Chester)
———— *What God Has Done Is Rightly Done.* Series I (Chester)
———— *Pan's Dancing Song.* Series II (Chester)
Bach-Siloti—*Organ Prelude in E Minor*
———— *Organ Prelude in G Minor*
Bach-Tausig—*Toccata and Fugue in D Minor*
Bauer, H.—*Tunes from the 18th Century* (Schirmer)
———— *Ye Sweet Retreat, Motley, Flourish*
Beach, H. H. A.—Op. 107. *Nocturne* (Church)
———— *Fireflies* (rapid thirds)
———— *Autumn*
Beethoven-Bauer—*Gavotte in F*
Brahms—Op. 4. *Scherzo*
———— Ballades, intermezzi, capriccios, rhapsodies, and sonatas.
Chopin—Impromptus, waltzes, polonaises, nocturnes, etudes, ballades, scherzos, preludes, barcarolle, and sonatas.
Czerny-Joseffy—*Toccata in C* (Schirmer)
D'Albert—Op. 16, No. 2. *Scherzo*
Debussy—*Nocturne*
———— *2 Arabesques*
———— *Reflections in the Water*
———— *La cathédrale engloutie*
Dóhnanyi—*4 Rhapsodies* (1 and 4 best) (Doblinger, Wien)
———— Op. 17. *Pastorale, Toccata, Pavane and Variations*
———— *Introduction and Fugue*
Fauré, G.—Op. 31. *Impromptu No. 2 in F Minor* (B. M. Co.)

—————— Op. 33, No. 3. *Nocturne in A Flat*
—————— *Nocturne in F Minor*
Grodzky—Op. 1. *Etude in F Minor*
Grünfeld—Op. 47, No. 3. *Etude à la Tarantella* (Bote & Bock)
—————— *Menuet*
Henselt—*Spring Song*
—————— Op. 12. *Concert Etudes*
Hutcheson, E.—*Capriccio*
—————— *Scherzo* from Mendelssohn's *Midsummer Night's Dream*
—————— *Ride of the Valkyries* (Wagner)
—————— Op. 10. *Scherzo, Capriccio, Sarabande*
Jonas, A.—*Toccata in A*
Jongen, J.—Op. 33. *Claire de lune*
—————— Op. 40. *2 Walloon Rounds* (Durand)
—————— Op. 52. *Crépuscule au Lac Ogwen* (Chester)
Leschetizky—Op. 44. *Intermezzo in Octaves*
—————— Op. 45. *Arabesque à la Tarentelle*
Liápounov—Op. 11. *Transcendental Etudes*
Liszt—*Waldesrauschen*
—————— *Gnomenreigen*
—————— *Etude in F Minor*
—————— *Paganini Caprices* (La Campanella, etc.)
—————— *Hungarian Rhapsodies*
—————— *Valse Impromptu*
—————— *Polonaise in E*
—————— *La Predication aux Oiseaux*
—————— *St. François de Paul Marchant sur les Flots*
—————— *Ballade No. 2*
—————— *At the Spring*
—————— *Venice and Naples*
Mendelssohn—*Rondo Capriccioso*
—————— *Variations Sérieuses*
Moskowski—Op. 27. *Barcarolle in G*
—————— Op. 27. *Tarentelle in G Flat*
—————— Op. 37. *Caprice Espagnol*
—————— Op. 24. *Etude in G Flat*
—————— Op. 32, No. 2. *Etude*
—————— *En Automne*
Napravnik—Op. 48, No. 2. *Scherzo*

———— *Nocturne* (reminiscent of Chopin)

Nicode—Op. 13, *Tarentelle*

———— Op. 13, No. 3. *Barcarolle*

Paderewski—Op. 14. *Caprice in the Style of Scarlatti*

———— Op. 16, No. 2. *Melody*

———— *Nocturne in B Flat*

———— Op. 5, No. 2. *Mazurka in E Minor*

———— Op. 16. *Two Legends*

———— *Theme and Variations in A Major*

———— Op. 11. *Theme and Variations in A Minor*

———— *Nocturne*

———— *Melody*

———— *Cracovienne*

Palmgren—*The Isle of Shadows*

———— *The Sea*

———— *Birds*

———— *Will o' the Wisp*

———— *May Night*

Pierné—*Allegro Scherzando*

———— *Prelude and Fugue*

———— *Cache-cache*

Poldini—*Japanese Etude*

Rachmaninoff—Op. 16, No. 15. *Moment Musical*

———— Op. 23. Preludes (G minor and G major)

———— *Prelude in C Sharp Minor*

———— *Valse*

———— *Humoresque*

———— *Melodie in E*

———— *Hopak*

———— Op. 10. *Nocturne*

———— *Menuet by Bizet*

———— *Etude Tableau*

Raff—Op. 157, No. 2. *La Fileuse*

———— *Fairy Tale* (*Märchen*)

Ravel—*Jeux d'eau*

———— *Pavane*

Reinhold—Op. 28, No. 2. *Impromptu in A Flat*

———— Op. 28, No. 3. *Impromptu in C Sharp Minor*

Rubinstein—Op. 10, No. 22. (Kammenoi-Ostrow)

———— Op. 30, No. 1. *Barcarolle in F Minor*

———— *Barcarolle in A Minor*

———— *Barcarolle in G Major*
———— *Barcarolle in F Minor*
———— *Barcarolle in A Minor*
———— *Etude on False Notes*
———— *Staccato Etude in C*
———— *Valse in E Flat*
Saint-Saëns—Op. 24, the 2nd Mazurka (Durand)
———— *Allegro Appassionata*
———— Op. 72. *Album for Pianoforte*
———— *Scherzo* (from *Midsummer Night's Dream*)
———— *Bourrée for Left Hand*
Sauer—*Près du Ruisseau* (Schott)
Scharwenka, X.—Op. 22, No. 1. *Novellette*
———— Op. 5, No. 1. *Erzählung*
———— Op. 31. *Waltz*
Schubert—Op. 90. *Impromptu in G Major*
Schubert-Liszt—*Auf dem Wasser zu Singen*
———— *Du bist die Ruh*
Schubert-Scharwenka—*Impromptu à la Hongroise* (B. & H.)
Schumann, G.—Op. 111. *Tarentelle*
Schumann, R.—Op. 12. *Fantasiestücke* (8 numbers)
———— Op. 82. *Forest Scenes*
———— Op. 28. *3 Romanzen*
———— *Novellettes*
———— *Kreisleriana*
———— Op. 9. *Carnaval*
———— Op. 26. *Faschingsschwank aus Wien*
———— *Davidsbündlertänze*
Schumann-Joseffy—*Toccata in C*
Sgambati—*Nocturne in B Minor*
———— Op. 31. *Nocturne in A Flat*
———— Op. 23. *Rappelle-Toi*
———— Op. 23. *Gigue*
———— Op. 18. *Toccata*
Sinding—Op. 32. *Marche Grotesque* (Peters)
———— *Caprice*
Sinigaglia, L.—Op. 11. *Staccato Etude*
Smetana—Op. 17. *By the Seashore*
Sternberg—Op. 103. *Etude in C Minor* (brilliant) (Schir-mer)
———— *Prélude and Bourrée*

Stojowski—*Chanson d'amour*
———— *Spinning Song* (Pitt & Halzfield)
Tchaikovsky—Op. 72, No. 5. *Méditation*
———— Op. 72. *Berceuse, Méditation, Mazurque pour danser*
———— Op. 4. *Valse Caprice*
———— Op. 10. *Nocturne*
———— Op. 1. *Impromptu*
Wagner-Brassin—*Magic Fire*
Wagner-Liszt—*Spinning Song* from *The Flying Dutchman*
Wagner-Tausig—*Sigmund's Love Song*

OCTAVE STUDIES

Biehl—Op. 140. *Easy Octave Studies*
Czerny—Op. 553. *Octave Studies*
Denee, C.—*Progressive Studies in Octaves* (A. P. Schmidt)
Döring—Op. 24. *School of Octaves* (with preparatory section) (Sch. C. Fischer. Wood)
———— Op. 25. *Advanced Octaves Studies*
Eggling, Geo.—Op. 90. *18 Octave Studies* (melodious)
Gurlitt—Op. 100. *24 Octave Studies* (Schirmer Library)
Herzog and Pinter—*Art of Octave Playing* (great variety from various composers) (C. Fischer)
Hugo, J. A.—*Octave Studies*
Langdon, C.—*Wrist Studies* (Presser)
Loeschhorn—*School of Octaves* (very complete; difficult passages; taken from celebrated compositions) (Peters)
Low, Jos.—Op. 281. *Octave Studies*
Ludwig, Ernst—Op. 16. *19 Octave Studies* (Universal)
Orth, A.—*18 Octave Studies* (Presser)
Paaly, Leo—*Technical Octave Studies* (Presser)
Pacher—Op. 11. *Octave Studies* (moderately difficult)
Perry, E. B.—*5 Wrist Studies* (no octaves) (C. W. Thompson)
Phillip—*Etudes d'Octaves d'après Bach, Clementi, etc.* (Durand)
———— *School of Octaves* (3 books: 1. Exercises 2. Ten original Studies 3. Examples, from Beethoven to the present) (Schirmer)

Presser—*First Studies in Octave Playing* (Presser)
Preyer, A.—Op. 30. *Octave Studies* (2 books; melodic) (Ditson)
Rogers, J. H.—*10 Octave Studies*
Sartorio—Op. 1105. *Studies Preparatory to Octave Playing* (Presser)
———— Op. 1012. *Pieces in Octaves* (Presser)
Smith, W. J.—*Thematic Octave Studies* (Presser)
Terry, Frances—*12 Artistic Studies*
Vogt, Jean—Op. 145. *Varied Styles of Octaves.* (Schirmer Library)
Wolff, B.—*12 Short Octave Studies for Equal Development* (Presser)
———— Op. 106. *Octave Studies*

CONCERT ETUDES IN OCTAVES

Beethoven—Saint-Saëns—*Dervishes* (Durand)
Bendel—Op. 27. *Etude in Sixths*
Brassin—*Scherzo d'après Scarlatti*
———— *Octaves and Thirds* (Schott)
Breitenfeld—*Octave Study* (Edition Strache)
Campbell-Tipton—Op. 30. *Etude in Octaves* (Schirmer)
Chopin—Op. 25. *Etude in Octaves*
Concone, J.—*Waltz in Octaves* (easy) (Schirmer)
Dóhnanyi—Op. 28. *Concert Etude IV*
Godard, B.—*En Route*
———— *Le Chevalier Fantastique* (Schirmer)
———— *Boniment* (Magic Lantern)
Grunfeldt, A.—*Octave Study in E* (difficult)
Leschetizky—*Intermezzo in Octaves* (brilliant and difficult)
Litolff—*Les Octaves* (Schirmer)
MacFayden—Op. 22. *Octave Etude* (Schirmer)
Moszkowski—*Concert Etude in C Major*
———— Op. 53, No. 4. *The Juggleress* (Peters)
Otterstrom—*Concert Etude No. 5 in E Major* (Hansen)
Pirkhert—*Octave Etude No. 16* (in *Nouveau Gradus*)
Raff—Op. 8, No. 9. *Gladiatori*
Rubinstein—*Etude in C Major* (staccato)
Sauer, E.—*Moto Perpetuo in Octaves* (Peters)

Scharwenka, X.—*Staccato Etude in E Flat*
Schultz-Elver—*Octave Study in G* (Jurgens, Moskow)
Speidel—Op. 18. No. 2. (Bahn, Berlin)

SETS OR GROUPS OF PIECES

Arensky—Op. 43. *Six Caprices* (Jurgensen)
Blanchet, Emile—Op. 18. *Caïques* (*Eiouk, Au Jardin du Vieux Serail*)
Cooke, J. F.—*Italian Lakes: Suite for Pianoforte* (*Beautiful Isle, Shadows on Lake Como, Jasmine and Nightingale, An Old Palace, Fire Dance*) (*Presser*)
D'Albert—Op. 1. *Suite* (*Allemande, Courante, Sarabande, Gavotte* and *Musette, Gigue*)
Debussy—*Pour le Piano* (*Prelude, Sarabande, Toccata*)
Dóhnanyi—Op. 17. *Humoresques* (Universal)
Dubois, T.—*Poèmes Alpestres* (*Vers les Cimes, Au Sommet, Le Chevrier, Le Chamois, La Neige, Le Vertige*) (Au Ménestrel)
———— *Poèmes Sylvestres* (*L'Allée Solitaire, Les Myrtilles, Les Bucherons, Le Banc de Mousse, La Source Enchantée, Danse Rustique*) (Durand)
Dvořák—*Silhouettes*
———— Op. 85. *Poetical Images* (3 vols) (Universal)
Gade, Niels W.—Op. 34. *Idylls* (*In the Flower Garden, By the Brook, Birds of Passage, Evening Twilight*) (moderately easy) (Augener)
Gernsheim—Op. 59, Book II (*Nocturne, Elegy, In the Rushes, Romanza, Aeolus*) (Rieter-Biedermann)
Jensen, A.—Op. 44. *Erotikon* (*Cassandra, The Enchantress, Galatea, Electra, Complaint of Adonis, Eros, Kypris*)
———— Op. 36. *German Suite in B Minor* (*Allemande, Courante, Sarabande, Gavotte and Musette, Gigue*) (Bahn, Berlin)
Kaun, Hugo—Op. 71. *Pierrot and Columbine* (*The Meeting, The Wooing, The Springtime of Love, The Quarrel and Reconciliation*) (Charlier, Berlin)
Klein, B. O.—Op. 25. *Suite* (*Prelude, Theme and Variations, Menuet, Elegy, Gavotte*) (Schirmer)
Lieurance, T.—*From the Dalles to Minnetonka* (Presser)
MacDowell—Op. 55. *Sea Pieces* (*To the Sea, From a Wan-*

dering Iceberg, A.D. 1620 (Landing of the Pilgrims), *Starlight, Song, From the Depths, Nautilus, In Mid-ocean*) (A. P. Schmidt)

—— Op. 10. *Suite (Praeludium, Fugato, Rhapsody, Scherzino, March, Fantastic Dance)*

—— Op. 19. *Forest Idylls (Forest Calmness, Play of the Nymphs, Revery, Dance of the Dryads)*

—— Op. 28. *Idylls* (6 pieces)

—— Op. 32. *Four Little Poems (The Eagle, The Brook, Moonshine, Winter)*

—— Op. 38. *Marionettes (Soubrette, The Lover, Knave, Sweetheart, Clown, Witch)*

Moor, E.—Op. 86. *Six Impressions* (Mathot)

Moussorgsky—*Tableaux d'une Exposition (Promenade, The Gnome, Chicks, Rich and Poor, The Market Place, Catacombs, The Old Witch, The City Gates)* (arr. by Harold Bauer) (Schirmer)

Niemann, Walter—*Lousiana Suite* (Presser)

Raff, J.—Op. 204. *Suite (Prelude, Sarabande, Rigadon, Menuet, Air, Tambourin)* (Charlier, Berlin)

Saint-Saens—Op. 72. *Album for Pianoforte (Prelude, Carillon, Toccata, Chanson Napolitaine, Wedding Cake, Finale)*

Schumann, Georg—Op. 27. *Harzbilder (An der Ilse, Von Hackelberg, Dem Wilden Jäger, Die Maer von der Rosstrappe, Ausblick in die Ferne, Nebel, Idyll)*

Schumann, R.—Op. 2. *Papillons* (Peters)

—— Op. 6. *Davidsbündlertänze*

—— Op. 13. *Etudes Symphoniques*

—— Op. 15. *Scenes from Childhood*

—— Op. 16. *Kreisleriana*

—— Op. 19. *Blumenstück*

—— Op. 20. *Humoreske*

—— Op. 23. *Nachtstücke*

—— Op. 26. *Faschingsschwank aus Wien*

—— Op. 28. *3 Romanzen*

—— Op. 82. *Forest Scenes*

Schütt, E.—Op. 48. *Carnaval Mignon (Prelude, Serenade d'Arlequin, Tristesse de Colombine, Polichinelle, Pierrot Reveur, Sganarelle)* (B. M. Co.)

—— Op. 43. *Three Piano Pieces*

—— Op. 45. *Causeries de bal*
—— Op. 35. *8 Preludes* (Rahter)
Schytte—Op. 79. *Miniatures* (2 vols)
Sjogren—Op. 15. *Auf der Wanderschaft*
—— Op. 10. *Erotikon*
Strong, T.—Op. 36. *4 Poems* (*Morning, In the Forest, Elegy, A Midsummer Night's Dream*) (B. & H.)
Tchaikovsky—Op. 37. *The Seasons* (*Before the Chimney, Carnival, Song of the Lark, The Snowdrop, Clear Nights, Barcarolle, Reaper's Song, The Harvest, Hunting Song, In Autumn, Troika Ride, Christmas*)

TRANSCRIPTIONS FOR PIANO SOLO

Albeniz-Godowski—*Tango*
Bach-Brahms—*Presto in G Minor* (Simrock)
Bach-Burmeister—*Rondo Gavotte* (6th violin sonata) (Ditson)
—— *Prelude in E Flat* (*The Well Tempered Clavier*) (Ditson)
Bach-Busoni—*Chorale Preludes* (2 books)
Bach-Hess—*Jesu, Joy of Man's Desiring* (Oxford Press)
Bach-Joseffy—*Overture, Air and Bourrée* (Schirmer)
Bach-Mannes—*Overture* (Schirmer)
Bach-Murdoch—*Organ Fugue in G Minor* (Schott)
—— *Organ Prelude and 2nd Fugue in C Minor* (Schott)
—— *Herr Christ, der einzige Gottes Sohn* (Schott)
—— *Sicilienne* (2nd flute sonata) (Schott)
—— *16 Choral Preludes* (4 books) (Schott)
Bach-Reger—*Prelude and Fugue in D Major* (B. & H.)
—— *Prelude and Fugue in E Flat* (B. & H.)
—— *Toccata and Fugue in D Minor* (B. & H.)
Bach-Rummel—*Seven Transcriptions* (Chester)
Bach-Tausig—*Toccata and Fugue in D*
Bauer, Harold—*Music of the Past* (Kirnberger, *Toccata;* Merulo, *Toccata;* Frescobaldi, *Capriccio on the Cuckoo's Call;* Kittel, *Nachspiel;* Matheson, *Air Varié, Menuet;* Muffat, *Sarabande, Fughetta;* Schobert, *Menuet, Capriccio*) (B. M. Co.)
Beethoven-Bauer—*Gavotte*
Beethoven-Saint-Saëns—*Dervish Dance*

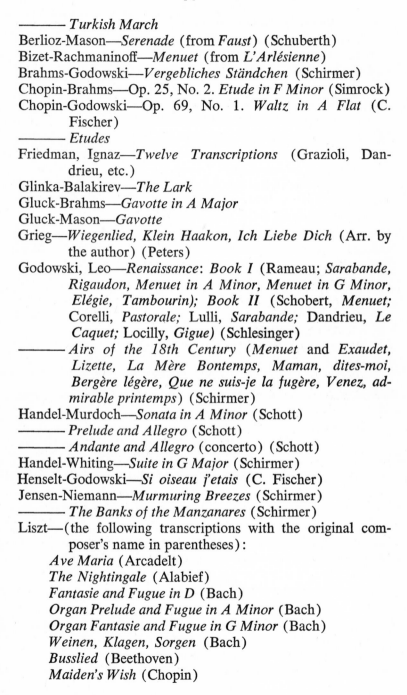

———— *Turkish March*

Berlioz-Mason—*Serenade* (from *Faust*) (Schuberth)

Bizet-Rachmaninoff—*Menuet* (from *L'Arlésienne*)

Brahms-Godowski—*Vergebliches Ständchen* (Schirmer)

Chopin-Brahms—Op. 25, No. 2. *Etude in F Minor* (Simrock)

Chopin-Godowski—Op. 69, No. 1. *Waltz in A Flat* (C. Fischer)

———— *Etudes*

Friedman, Ignaz—*Twelve Transcriptions* (Grazioli, Dandrieu, etc.)

Glinka-Balakirev—*The Lark*

Gluck-Brahms—*Gavotte in A Major*

Gluck-Mason—*Gavotte*

Grieg—*Wiegenlied, Klein Haakon, Ich Liebe Dich* (Arr. by the author) (Peters)

Godowsky, Leo—*Renaissance: Book I* (Rameau; *Sarabande, Rigaudon, Menuet in A Minor, Menuet in G Minor, Elégie, Tambourin); Book II* (Schobert, *Menuet;* Corelli, *Pastorale;* Lulli, *Sarabande;* Dandrieu, *Le Caquet;* Locilly, *Gigue)* (Schlesinger)

———— *Airs of the 18th Century* (*Menuet* and *Exaudet, Lizette, La Mère Bontemps, Maman, dites-moi, Bergère légère, Que ne suis-je la fugère, Venez, admirable printemps*) (Schirmer)

Handel-Murdoch—*Sonata in A Minor* (Schott)

———— *Prelude and Allegro* (Schott)

———— *Andante and Allegro* (concerto) (Schott)

Handel-Whiting—*Suite in G Major* (Schirmer)

Henselt-Godowski—*Si oiseau j'etais* (C. Fischer)

Jensen-Niemann—*Murmuring Breezes* (Schirmer)

———— *The Banks of the Manzanares* (Schirmer)

Liszt—(the following transcriptions with the original composer's name in parentheses):

Ave Maria (Arcadelt)

The Nightingale (Alabief)

Fantasie and Fugue in D (Bach)

Organ Prelude and Fugue in A Minor (Bach)

Organ Fantasie and Fugue in G Minor (Bach)

Weinen, Klagen, Sorgen (Bach)

Busslied (Beethoven)

Maiden's Wish (Chopin)

My Repose (Chopin)
Chant Polonaise (Chopin)
Faust Waltz (Gounod)
Maid of the Ganges (Mendelssohn)
Wedding March and Elfin Song (Mendelssohn)
On Wings of Song (Mendelssohn)
La Campanella (Paganini)
Six Grand Etudes (Paganini)
Venetian Regatta (Rossini)
Der Asra (Rubinstein)
My Repose (Schubert)
Auf dem Wasser (Schubert)
Hark, Hark the Lark (Schubert)
Am Meer (Schubert)
Ave Maria (Schubert)
Soirées de Vienne (Schubert)
Serenade (Schubert)
Erl King (Schubert)
Spring Night (Schumann)
Dedication (Schumann)
Linden Tree (Schubert)
The Wanderer (Schubert)
Meine Ruhe ist hin (Schubert)
Rigoletto Fantasie (Verdi)
Don Juan Fantasie (Mozart)
Liebestod from *Tristan* (Wagner)
Senta's Ballade from *The Flying Dutchman* (Wagner)
Entrance of the Guests from *Tannhäuser* (Wagner)
Evening Star from *Tannhäuser* (Wagner)
Pilgrim Chorus from *Tannhäuser* (Wagner)
March to the Holy Grail from *Parsifal* (Wagner)
Elsa's Dream from *Lohengrin* (Wagner)
Elsa's Bridal Procession from *Lohengrin* (Wagner)
Festspiel and *Brautlied* from *Lohengrin* (Wagner)
Spinning Song from *The Flying Dutchman* (Wagner)
Frühlings Glaube (Schubert)
Wohin (Schubert)
Du bist die Ruh (Schubert)
Mendelssohn-Heller—*On Wings of Song*
Mozart-Backhaus—*Serenade* (from *Don Juan*)
Mozart-Boscowitz—*Menuet in E Flat*

Moussorgsky-Rachmaninoff—*Hopak*
Rimski-Korsakov-Rachmaninoff—*Flight of the Bumblebee*
    (Schott)
Saint-Saëns-Godowski—*Le Cygne*
Schubert-Ganz—Ballet music from *Rosamunde*
Schubert-Godowski—*By the Sea* (Schirmer)
————— *Trockene Blumen* (Schirmer)
————— *Ballet* (from *Rosamunde*)
————— *Impatience*
————— *Gute Nacht*
Schubert-Rachmaninoff—*The Brook*
Schubert-Scharwenka—*Impromptu à la Hongroise* (B.&H.)
Schubert-Tausig—*Military March*
Schumann-Godowski—*A Highland Cradle Song* (Schirmer)
Schumann-Tausig—*Der Kontrobandist* (Bote & Bock)
Schütt-Godowski—*Russian Song* (Schirmer)
Strauss-Backhaus—*Serenade*
Strauss-Beach—*Serenade*
Strauss-Godowski—*Serenade*
Wagner-Brassin—*Magic Fire*
————— *Waldweben*
Wagner-Rubinstein—*Siegfried and the Rhinedaughters*
    (Schott)
Wagner-Tausig—*Siegmund's Liebeslied*
Weber-Brahms—*Perpetual Motion* (for left hand alone)
    (Simrock)

VARIATIONS FOR PROGRAMS

Bach, J. S.—*Goldberg Variations*
————— *Aria Variata alla Maniera Italiana* (Steingraber)
Beethoven—*32 Variations in C Minor*
————— *Variations in F Major*
————— *Variations in G Major on Nel Cor Piu* (easy)
————— *3 Variations from a Youthful Period* (easy)
Bizet—*Variations Chromatiques* (Choudens)
Brahms—Op. 9. *Variations on a Schumann Theme*
    (Augener)
————— Op. 21, No. 1. *Variations on an Original Theme*
————— Op. 21, No. 2. *Variations on a Hungarian Theme*
————— Op. 24. *Variations on a Handel Theme* (Augener)

———— Op. 35. *Paganini Variations* (very difficult)

———— Op. 56. *Variations on a Haydn Theme*

Casella, A.—*Variations sur une Chaconne* (A. X. Mathot)

Chevillard, C.—Op. 5. *Theme and Variations* (Enoch & Sons)

Chopin—Op. 2. *La Ci Darem la Mano*

———— Op. 12. *Je Vends de Scapulaires*

Fauré—Op. 73. *Theme and Variations* (B. M. Co).

Freyer, H.—Op. 21. *Six Variations on a Rigadoon by Purcell* (Schott)

Gabrilowitch—Op. 4. (Zimmermann)

Greenop, E.—*Air and Variations* (Chester)

Grieg—*Ballade* (difficult) (Peters)

Handel—*Variations in E Major* (*The Harmonious Blacksmith*)

———— *Air with Variations in B Flat*

———— *2 Chaconnes with Variations in G Major*

Haydn—*Variations in F Minor*

Heller—Op. 142. *Theme and Variations on Schumann's "Warum"* (B. & H.)

Mandyczewski—Op. 5. *Variations on a Handel Theme* (Universal)

———— Op. 6. *10 Variations on a Handel Theme* (Universal)

Matheson, J.—*Sarabande with 3 Variations*

Mendelssohn—Op. 54. *17 Variations Sérieuses*

———— Op. 82. *Variations in E Flat*

———— Op. 83. *Variations in B Flat*

Mozart—*Variations in F* (Siloti) (C. Fischer)

———— *Pastorale Variée*

———— *Sonata in A Major* (1st part)

Murschhauser—*Aria Pastoralis Variata*

Pachulski, H.—Op. 1. *Variations* (Schirmer)

Paderewski—Op. 11. *Variations and Fugue in A Minor* (Bote & Bock)

———— Op. 16, No. 3 (in A major) (Schirmer)

Pierné, G.—Op. 30. *Pastorale Variée* (from *Ecole Moderne du Piano,* Book IV) (Durand)

Rachmaninoff—Op. 42. *Variations on a Theme by Corelli* (C. Fischer)

Rameau—*Les Niais de Sologne*

———— *Gavotte and Variations*

Royce, E.—*Theme and Variations in A Minor* (Schirmer)

Rubinstein, A.—Op. 88. *Variations in G*

―――― Op. 104. *Variations in A Flat*

Saint-Saëns—Op. 97. *Thème Varié*

Schafer, Kirk—*Variationen auf eine Sequenz* (Kahnt, Leipzig)

Scharwenka—Op. 57. *Variations on a Theme by C. H.* (Bote & Bock)

Schelling, E.—*Theme and Variations in F Sharp Minor* (Schirmer)

Schubert—*Impromptu and Variations in B Flat*

Schumann, G.—Op. 61. *Theme and Variations*

―――― Op. 64. *Variations and Fugue on an Original Theme*

Schumann, R.—Op. 1. *Abegg Variations*

―――― Op. 13. *Etudes Symphoniques*

Schütt, E.—Op. 29. *Thème Varié et fugato* (Simrock)

―――― Op. 62. *Thème Varié* (Simrock)

―――― *A Russian Song* (easy) (Schirmer)

Sinding, C.—Op. 94. *Fatum Variations*

Sjogren—Op. 48. *Theme and Variations* (Hansen)

Tchaikovsky—Op. 19. *Theme and Variations*

Von Fielitz—Op. 90. *Thème Varié* (B. & H.)

Von Weber—*Variations on an Air* (from *Joseph*) (Peters)

Zipoli—*Partita (Boghen)* (Ricordi)

CONCERTOS WITH ORCHESTRA

Bach, J. S.—*Concerto in C* (3 pianos and strings)

―――― *Concerto in F Minor*

―――― *Concerto in D*

―――― *Concerto in A Minor*

―――― *Concerto in E*

―――― *Concerto in D Minor*

―――― *Concerto in A Minor* (4 pianos) (B. & H.)

―――― *Concerto in C Minor* (2 pianos and string orchestra) (B. & H.)

―――― *Concerto in C Minor* (2 pianos, arr. by Harold Bauer) (Schirmer)

Bach, W. F.—*Concerto in F* (2 pianos)

―――― *Concerto in E Flat* (2 pianos)

―――― *Concerto in E Minor*

―――― *Concerto in A Minor*

―――― *Concerto in D Major*

———— *Concerto in E Major*
Bach, J. Chr.—*Concerto in G Major*
———— *Concerto in E Major*
———— *Concerto in D Major*
Bach, K. P. E.—*Concerto in C Minor*
———— *Concerto in G Major*
———— *Concerto in E Flat Major*
Boyle, George—*Concerto D Minor* (Schirmer)
Brahms—Op. 15. *Concerto No. 1 in D Minor* (very difficult)
———— Op. 83. *Concerto No. 2 in B Flat Major*
Beethoven—*Concerto in B Flat* (the easiest)
———— *Concerto in C Major*
———— *Concerto in C Minor*
———— *Concerto in G Major*
———— *Concerto in E Flat Major* (The Emperor)
Brassin—Op. 22. *Concerto in F* (B. & H.)
Cleve, Halfdan—Op. 3. *Concerto in A Major* (B. & H.)
Carpenter, J. A.—*Concertino*
Chopin—Op. 11. *Concerto in E Minor*
———— Op. 21. *Concerto in F Minor*
Chausson—Op. 21. *Concerto in D Major* (solo piano, solo
    violin, and string quartet) (Rouart)
Delius—*Concerto*
D'Albert—Op. 12. *Concerto in E Major*
Dussek—Op. 63. (2 pianos, rather easy)
Godard—Op. 31. *Concerto in A Minor* (Bote & Bock)
Gradstein, Alfred—*Concerto No. 1*
Grieg—Op. 16. *Concerto in Minor* (Peters)
Hadley, H. K.—*Concertino*
Handel—2 *Concertos, G Minor and F Major* (Steingraber)
Hauptmann—Op. 20. *Concerto.*
Haydn—*Concerto in D Major* (easy) (Steingraber)
Henselt—Op. 16. *F Minor Concerto*
Hiller—Op. 69. *F Sharp Minor Concerto*
Hochberg, Graf von—Op. 42. *Concerto* (Simrock)
Kalkbrenner—Op. 125. *Concerto for 2 pianos* (rather easy)
Liszt—*E Flat Concerto* (brilliant and difficult)
———— *A Minor Concerto*
———— *Concerto Pathetique* (2 pianos alone)
MacDowell—Op. 15. *A Minor Concerto*
———— Op. 28. *D Minor Concerto*

Marx, J.—*Concerto Romantique* (Universal)
Mayer, Carl—Op. 70. *D Major Concerto*
Mendelssohn—Op. 25. *G Minor Concerto*
———— Op. 40. *D Minor Concerto*
Moeschinger, A.—Op. 23. *Concerto No. 2* (chamber orchestra) (Schott)
Moor, E.—Op. 85. *Concerto* (Mathot)
Moscheles, Ignaz—Op. 58. *G Minor Concerto* (excellent study) (Klemm, Leipzig)
Moszkowski—Op. 59. *E Major Concerto* (Peters)
Mozart, W.—*B Flat Concerto* (one of the easier of the 25 concertos)
———— *A Major Concerto* (a favorite)
———— *D Minor Concerto* (another favorite)
————*D Major Concerto* (Coronation)
———— *E Flat Concerto* (2 pianos) (Steingraber)
Paderewski—Op. 17. *A Minor Concerto* (Bote & Bock)
Palmgren—Op. 33. *The River* (fine)
Rachmaninoff—*Concerto No. 1.*
———— *Concerto No. 2* (C minor) (Gutheil)
———— *Concerto No. 3.*
Raff—Op. 185. *C Minor Concerto*
Rameau—*5 Concertos* (Steingraber)
Ravel—*Concerto for the Left Hand Alone*
———— *Concerto* (Durand)
Reinecke, Carl—Op. 72. *F Sharp Minor Concerto*
Rheinberger, J.—Op. 94. *Concerto for 2 pianos* (6 hands) (Schott)
Ries—Op. 55. *C Sharp Minor Concerto* (B. & H.)
Rimski-Korsakov—Op. 30. *C Sharp Minor Concerto*
Rosenhein—Op. 73. *Concerto* (moderately difficult)
Rubinstein, A.—Op. 45. *Concerto No. 3* (G Major)
————Op. 70. *Concerto No. 4* (D minor, the favorite)
Saint-Saëns—Op. 17. *D Major Concerto* (No. 1)
———— Op. 22. *G Minor Concerto* (No. 2)
————Op. 29. *E Minor Concerto* (No. 3)
———— Op. 44. *C Minor Concerto* (No. 4)
Scharwenka, X. Op. 56. *C Minor Concerto*
———— *B Flat Minor Concerto* (scherzo arr. for 2 pianos)
Schumann, R—Op. 54. *A Minor Concerto* (Schott)
Schütt, E.—Op. 7. *G Minor Concerto* (Simrock)

——— Op. 47. *F Minor Concerto* (Simrock)
Schytte—Op. 28. *C Sharp Minor Concerto* (Hainauer)
Scott, Cyril—*Concerto* (Schott)
Sgambati—Op. 15. *Concerto* (Schott)
Stenhammer—Op. 1. *B Minor Concerto* (Hainauer)
Stojowski—*F Sharp Minor Concerto* (Augener)
Taubert—Op. 18. *E Flat Concerto*
Tchaikovsky—Op. 23. *Concerto in B Flat* (No. 1) (favorite)
——— Op. 44. *Concerto in G* (No. 2)
——— Op. 75. *Concerto in E Flat* (No. 3)
Tcherepnin—*Concerto for Piano, Flute and Violin* (Schott)
Thalberg—Op. 5. *F Minor Concerto*
Wieniawski—Op. 20. *G Minor Concerto*
Winding—Op. 16. *A Minor Concerto*
Wladerikoff—*Concerto*

COMPOSITIONS FOR TWO AND THREE PIANOS

Bach, J. S.—*Concerto in C Minor* (with string orchestra)
  (B. & H.)
——— Same (arr. by Harold Bauer without orchestra)
  (Schirmer)
——— *Concerto in C* (3 pianos, 6 hands)
Bach, W. F.—*Concerto in F*
——— *Concerto in E Flat*
Beethoven—*Triple Concerto* (piano, violin, cello, and orchestra)
Dussek—Op. 63. (easy)
Juon, P.—*Triple Concerto* (piano, violin, cello, and orchestra)
Kalkbrenner—Op. 125. (easy)
Liszt—*Concerto Pathetique* (no orchestra)
Rheinberger—Op. 94. (2 pianos, 6 hands)

CONCERT PIECES

Aubert, L.—Op. 8. *Fantasie* (Durand)
Chopin—Op. 22. *Andante Spianato and Polonaise in E Flat*
——— Op. 2. *La Ci Darem la Mano Variations*
——— Op. 13. *Grande Fantasie on Polish Airs*
——— Op. 14. *Krakoviak*
De Falla—*The Gardens of Spain*

Franck—*Variations Symphoniques* (solo) (Litolff)
Gaillard, M. F.—*Images d'Epinal* (chamber orchestra)
Godard—Op. 49. *Introduction and Allegro* (Durand)
Harsanyi, Tibor—*Konzertstück* (Senart)
Hure, J.—*Nocturne* (Mathot)
Liszt—*Ungarische Fantasie* (Schirmer)
Mendelssohn—Op. 22. *Capriccio in B Minor*
—————— Op. 29. *Rondo Brilliante*
Menter, Sophie—*Ungarische Zigeunerweisen* (Schirmer)
Reinecke, C.—Op. 33. *Concert Piece* (small orchestra)
Saint-Saëns—Op. 70. *Allegro Appassionato*
—————— Op. 73. *Rhapsodie d'Auvergne*
Schubert, F.—Op. 15. *Fantasie in C Major*
Schumann, R.—Op. 92. *Introduction and Allegro Appassionata*
—————— Op. 134. *Introduction and Concert Allegro*
Schütt, E.—Op. 56. *Fantasie*
—————— Op. 79. *Andante and Finale*
Strauss, R.—*Burleske in D* (Steingraber)
Tchaikovsky—Op. 56. *Fantasie de Concert*
—————— Op. 79. *Andante and Finale*
Weber, von—*Konzertstück in F Minor* (Peters)

CADENZAS TO CLASSICAL CONCERTOS
MOZART

Concerto No. 1—(F) *Cadenza* (last movement); C. Reinecke, Op. 87, No. 21 (B. & H.)
" No. 2—(B flat) *Cadenza,* C. Reinecke, Op. 87, No. 22 (B. & H.)
" No. 3—(D) *Cadenza,* C. Reinecke, Op. 87, No. 23
" No. 4—(G) *Cadenza* (1st and 3rd movements), C. Reinecke, Op. 87, Nos. 26-27 (B. & H.)
" No. 5—(D) *3 Cadenzas,* C. Reinecke, Op. 87, Nos. 28-30 (B. & H.)
" No. 5—(D) *3 Cadenzas,* Mozart
" No. 6—(B flat) *Cadenzas* (1st, 2d and 3d movements), C. Reinecke, Op. 87, Nos. 31-33 (B. & H.)
" No. 7—(F) 3 pianos
" No. 8—(C) *Cadenzas* (1st and 2d movements),

C. Reinecke, Op. 87, Nos. 34-35 (B. & H.)

" No. 9—(E flat) *Cadenzas* (1st and 2d movements), C. Reinecke, Op. 87, Nos. 36-37 (B. & H.)

" No. 9—(E flat)*Cadenzas*, Mozart

" No. 10—(E flat) 2 pianos, *Cadenzas* (1st and 3rd movements), C. Reinecke, Op. 87, Nos. 12-13 (B. & H.)

" No. 10—*Cadenzas* (1st and 3d movements), Ed. Mertke (Steingraber)

" No. 10—*Cadenzas* (1st and 3d movements), Reynaldo Hahn (Heugel)

" No. 10—*Cadenzas* (1st and 3d movements), Godowski

" No. 11—(F) (1st and last movements), C. Reinecke, Op. 87, Nos. 38-39 (B. & H.)

" No. 12—(A) *Cadenzas*, Mozart

" No. 13—(C) *Cadenzas*, C. Reinecke, Op. 87, No. 24

" No. 13—(C) *Cadenzas*, Mozart

" No. 14—(E flat) *Cadenzas* (1st and last movements), Geo. Schumann, Op. 69 (Leuckhart)

" No. 14—(E flat) *Cadenzas*, Hummel

" No. 14—(E flat) *Cadenzas*, Saint-Saëns (Durand)

" No. 15—(B flat) *Cadenzas* (1st and last movements), C. Reinecke, Op. 87, Nos. 18-19 (B. & H.)

" No. 15—(B flat) *Cadenzas*, Mozart

" No. 16—(D) *Cadenzas*, Mozart (B. & H.)

" No. 17—(G) *Cadenzas*, Mozart (B. & H.)

" No. 18—(B flat) *Cadenzas*, Mozart (B. & H.)

" No. 19—(F) *Cadenzas* (1st and last movements), Mozart (B. & H.)

" No. 20—(D minor) *Cadenzas* (1st and last movements), C. Reinecke, Op. 87, Nos. 16-17 (B. & H.)

" No. 20—*Cadenzas* (1st and last movements), Beethoven (B. & H.)

" No. 20—*Cadenzas* (1st and last movements), Zweigelt

" No. 20—*Cadenza* (1st and last movements), A. Casella

" No. 21—(C) *Cadenza*, C. Reinecke, Op. 87, No. 1

" No. 22—(E flat) *Cadenzas* (1st and last move-

ments), C. Reinecke, Op. 87, No. 41-42 (B. & H.)
" No. 22—(E flat) *Cadenzas* (1st and last movements), B. Marx-Goldschmidt (Simrock)
" No. 23—(A major) *Cadenza*, C. Reinecke, Op. 87, No. 11
" No. 23—(A major) *Cadenza*, Geo. Schumann, Op. 69 (Leuckhart)
" No. 23—(A major) *Cadenza*, Mozart
" No. 24—(C minor) *Cadenza*, C. Reinecke, Op. 87, No. 20 (B. & H.)
" No. 24—(C minor) *Cadenza*, Reynaldo Hahn (Heugel)
" No. 25—(G) *Cadenza*, C. Reinecke, Op. 87, No. 5
" No. 26—(D major) *Cadenza*, (1st movement), C. Reinecke, Op. 87, No. 2
" No. 26—(D major) *Cadenza*, Mozart
" No. 27—(B flat) *Cadenzas* (1st and last movements), C. Reinecke, Op. 87, No. 14-15
" No. 27—(B flat) *Cadenzas*, (1st and last movements), Mozart
" No. 28—(D) *Cadenza*, C. Reinecke, Op. 87, No. 40 (B. & H.)
" No. 28—(D) *Cadenza*, Mozart

BEETHOVEN

Concerto No. 1 in C, Op. 15—*Cadenzas* (1st and last movements), C. Reinecke, Op. 87, Nos. 6-7
" No. 1 in C. Op. 15—*Cadenzas* (1st and last movements), J. Moscheles (Simrock)
" No. 2 in B flat, Op. 19—*Cadenza* (1st movement), C. Reinecke, Op. 87, No. 25
" No. 2 in B flat, Op. 19—*Cadenza* (1st movement) J. Moscheles (Simrock)
" No. 2 in B flat, Op. 19—*Cadenza* (1st movement), Beethoven (Schirmer)
" No. 3 in C minor, Op. 37—*Cadenza*, C. Reinecke, Op. 87, No. 3 (B. & H.)
" No. 3 in C minor, Op. 37—*Cadenza*, J. Moscheles (Simrock)
" No. 3 in C minor, Op. 37—*Cadenza*, M. Levitzki

" No. 3 in C minor, Op. 37—*Cadenza*, Winding (Wm. Hansen)

" No. 3 in C minor, Op. 37—*Cadenza*, Harold Bauer (Ditson)

" No. 3 in C minor, Op. 37—*Cadenza*, Mrs. H. H. A. Beach, Op. 3

" No. 3 in C minor, Op. 37—*Cadenza*, Beethoven (Schirmer)

" No. 4 in G major, Op. 58—*Cadenza* (1st and last movements), George Schumann, Op. 69 (Leuckhart)

" No. 4 in G major, Op. 58—*Cadenza* (1st and last movements), Saint-Saëns (Durand)

" No. 4 in G major, Op. 58—*Cadenza* (1st and last movements), Jadassohn (B. & H.)

" No. 4 in G major, Op. 58—*Cadenza* (1st and last movements), C. Reinecke, Op. 87, Nos. 9-10 (B. & H.)

" No. 4 in G major, Op. 58—*Cadenza* (1st and last movements), J. Moscheles (Simrock)

MODERN SONATAS FOR CONCERT USE

Balákirev—*Sonata in B Flat Minor* (Universal)
Beethoven—A wide choice
Brahms—Op. 2. *Sonata in F Sharp Minor*
Campbell-Tipton—*Tragic Sonata*
Chopin—*Sonata in C Minor*
———— *Sonata in B Flat Minor*
———— *Sonata in B Minor*
Glázounov—Op. 27. *Second Sonata*
Godard—Op. 94. *Sonata in F Minor*
Gretchanínov—Op. 110. *Sonata No. 2* (Schott)
Grieg—Op. 7. *Sonata in E Minor* (Peters)
Griffes—Op. 14. *Sonata in F Minor* (Schirmer)
Krenek, E.—Op. 59. *Sonata No. 2* (Universal)
Liápounov—Op. 27
Liszt—*Sonata in B Minor*
MacDowell—Op. 45. *First Sonata (Tragica)*
————Op. 50. *Second Sonata (Eroica)*
————Op. 57. *Third Sonata (Norse)*

————Op. 59. *Fourth Sonata (Keltic)*
MacFayden—Op. 21. (Schirmer)
Niemann, Walter—Op. 60. *First Sonata (Romantic)*
———— Op. 75. *Second Sonata (Northern)*
———— Op. 83. *Third Sonata (Elegiac)*
Powell, J.—Op. 21. *Sonata in D* (B. M. & Co.)
Ravel—*Sonatine*
Rheinberger—Op. 135. *Sonata in E Flat Major*
Schumann—Op. 11, No. 1. *Sonata in F Sharp Minor*
———— Op. 22, No. 2. *Sonata in G Minor*
Schubert-Krenek—*Sonata* (Universal)
Schuloff, Erwin—*Sonata No. 1* (Universal)
Scriábin—Op. 23. *Sonata in F Sharp Minor*
———— Op. 30. *Sonata in F Sharp*
Sinding—Op. 91.
Soro, E.—*Sonata* (Schirmer)
Tchaikovsky—Op. 37. *Sonata in G*
Weber, von—Op. 49. *3rd Sonata* (final rondo nice)

CONCERT PIECES FOR THE LEFT HAND ALONE

Bach-Brahms—*Violin Chaconne* (Vol. II, Brahms' Studies)
     (Simrock)
Bach-Parsons—*Solfeggietto*
Gabrilówitsch—Op. 12, No. 2. *Etude.*
Godowski—*Impromptu for the Left Hand Alone*
———— *Suite for the Left Hand* (Schirmer)
———— *Waltz Poem No. III (Meditation)*
Gurlitt—Op. 185, No. 4. *Gavotte*
Hollander, A.—Op. 31. *Ten Left Hand Studies* (Schlesinger)
Hummel—Op. 43. *Left Hand Studies* (2 books)
Pauer, E.—*Suite for Left Hand* (Augener)
Piano Pieces for the Left Hand Alone (Spindler, *Romanza;*
     Hummel, *March;* Hollander, A., *Evening Song, The
     Hunt, Waltz;* Scriábin, *Prelude, Nocturne;* Donizetti-
     Leschetizki, Sextet from *Lucia*) (Boston Music Co.)
Pirkert—Op. 10, No. 5. *Theme*
Reger—*Four Left Hand Studies* (Universal)
Rheinberger—Op. 113. (*Menuet, Capriccio, Mazurka, Ro-
     mance, Gavotte*)
Saint-Saëns—Op. 135. *Six Pieces* (*Prelude, Alla Fuga, Moto*

Perpetuo, Bourrée, Elégie, Gigue) (Durand)
Schuloff—Op. 13, No. 5. *Left Hand Etude*
Spindler—Op. 350, No. 2. *Trauermarsch*
Spross—*Song Without Words*
Tappert, W.—*50 Exercises for Left Hand Alone* (2 books)
    (Simrock)
Thibault—*L'Ora Santa*
Van Eyken, H.—Op. 8. *Romance for Left Hand* (Simrock)
Weber-Brahms—*Perpetual Movement*
Weber-Tchaikovsky—*Perpetual Movement*

BARCAROLLES

Chopin—*Barcarolle in F Sharp* (difficult) (B. M. Co.)
Debussy—*En Bateau*
Falkenberg—*En Gondole* (Ecole Mod. II)
Fauré—*Eight Barcarolles* (Op. 26, 41, 42, 44, 66, 70, 90, 96)
Godard—*Venetienne* (4 barcarolles) (Schirmer)
Henselt—*La Gondola*
Jensen—*Barcarolle in A Flat* (easy)
Lavignac—*Barcarolle* (Ecole Mod. II)
Leschetizky—Op. 11, No. 4. *Barcarolle Venetienne*
Liadov—Op. 44. *Barcarolle in F Sharp Major*
Liszt—*Gondoliera* (in F Sharp, on an ancient Venetian
    Song)
Mendelssohn—*Gondellied* (Songs without Words, No. 29)
    (easy)
Moszkowski—Op. 41. *Gondoliera*
———— Op. 27, No. 1. *Barcarolle in G* (difficult)
Nicode—*Barcarolle*
Niemann, W.—Op. 94, No. 1. *Venezia* (Simrock)
Offenbach-Fischoff—*Barcarolle* (from *Tales from Hoffmann*)
    (Universal)
Offenbach-Gruenberg—*Barcarolle* (A. M. P.)
Offenbach-Moszkowski—*Barcarolle* (from *Tales from Hoff-
    mann)* (Peters)
Pacher—Op. 26. *Barcarolle* (from Meyerbeer's *Star of the
    North*) (easy)
Rachmaninoff—Op. 10, No. 3. *Barcarolle in G Minor*
    (Schirmer)
Rheinhold—Op. 34. *Barcarolle* (easy)
Richter—*Gondellied* (in F sharp minor) (easy)

Roger-Ducasse—*Barcarolle* (Ecole Mod. IV)
Rubinstein—*Five Barcarolles* (F minor, G major, G minor,
A minor, A major) (Augener)
Schubert-Liszt—*Auf dem Wasser zu Singen*
Sternberg—*Sulla Laguna* (easy)
Tchaikovsky—Op. 36, No. 6. *June* (Schirmer)

BALLADES

Bortkiewicz—Op. 42. *Ballade* (Litolff)
Brahms—*Four Ballades* (D major, D minor, B major, G minor)
Chopin—Op. 4. *Ballades* (F major, *Pastorale;* G minor, *Tragic; A* flat major, *Lyric;* F minor)
Cleve, Halfden—Op. 4. *Ballade* (B. & H.)
D'Albert—Op. 4. *Ballade*
Debussy—*Ballade*
Ehlert, L.—Op. 34. *Ballade*
Fauré, G.—Op. 19. *Ballade*
Friedmann, E.—Op. 66. *Ballade*
Grieg—Op. 24. *Ballade in G Minor* (Peters)
Liadov—Op. 21. *Ballade* (Balaieff)
Liszt—*Ballade in B Minor*
Philipp—Op. 6
Raff—Op. 74, No. 1
Reinecke, C.—*Ballade in A Flat*
Rheinberger, Jos.—*Ballade in G Minor* (excellent left hand study)
Scharwenka—Op. 8. *Ballade*
Schumann, G.—Op. 65. *Ballade*
Sibelius, Jean—*Ballade* (from *King Kristian Suite,* Part III)
Wertheimer, J. von—Op. 11
Wieniawski—Op. 31, *Ballade in E Flat Minor*
Yamada, Kosaka—*Japanese Ballade* (Schirmer)

TOCCATAS

Bach—*Toccata in G*
———— *Toccata in G* (arr. by Harold Bauer)
Bach-Tausig—*Toccata and Fugue in D Minor*
Balakirev—*Toccata in C Sharp Minor*
Bennett, Sterndale—*Toccata*

Czerny—*Toccata in C*
Czerny-Joseffy—*Toccata in C*
Czerny-Moszkowski—*Toccata in C*
Clementi—*Toccata in B Flat*
Debussy—*Toccata* (from *Pour le Piano*)
Dóhnanyi—Op. 11. *Toccata*
Gedalge—*Toccata in C Minor* (Enoch & Sons)
Henselt—*Toccatina*
Jonas—*Toccata in A*
Krenek—Op. 13. *Toccata and Chaconne*
Lachner—*Prelude and Toccata*
Lacombe—*Toccatina in A Major* (Durand)
Mason, William—*Toccatina in A Flat*
Massenet—*Modern French Composers* (Ditson)
Paderewski—Op. 6. *Introduction and Toccata*
Paradies—*Toccata in A*
Poldini—*Toccata* (Augener)
Prokofiev—Op. 11. *Toccata* (Universal)
Ravel—*Toccata* (from *Tombeau de Couperin*, No. 6)
Reinecke—*Toccatina in A Minor* (easy)
Rheinberger—*Prelude and Toccata in F Minor*
———— *Toccatina*
———— Op. 104. *Toccata in E Minor*
Saint-Saëns—Op. 72. *Toccata*
Schumann, R.— *Toccata in C Major*
Sgambati—*Toccata in A Flat*
Winding—*Toccata in F Minor*

CONCERT ETUDES

Brassin—*Concert Etude in D Flat* (Bahn, Berlin)
Chopin—Op. 10
———— Op. 25
———— *Three Posthumous Etudes*
Chopin-Moszkowski—*Waltz in D Flat*
Chopin-Philipp—*Waltz in D Flat*
Dóhnanyi—*Capriccio*
Glazounov—Op. 31, No. 3. *La Nuit* (Etude) (Schuberth)
Grodzki—Op. 1, No. 1. *Etude* (Schirmer)
Grunfeld—Op. 47. *Etude à la Tarantella*
Henselt—Op. 2, No. 12 (Joseffy) (Schirmer)

———— *If I Were a Bird*
Hiller—*Rhythmic Etude* (Bahn, Berlin)
Liápounov—Op. 11. *Etudes de Concert (Berceuse, Carillon, Nuit d'Eté, Idylle, Ronde des Fantômes, Terek, Tempête)*
Liszt—*Waldesrauschen*
———— *Gnomenreigen*
———— *Etude in D Flat* (II Sospiro)
———— *Etude in F Minor*
———— *Twelve Transcendental Etudes* (Schirmer)
MacDowell—Op. 36. *Concert Etude in F Sharp Major*
Mendelssohn—Op. 104. *Etude in F*
———— Op. 104. *Etude in B Flat Minor*
Moszkowski—Op. 24, No. 3. *Etude in C Major*
———— *Les Vagues*
———— Op. 64. *Advanced Etudes in Double Notes* (B. & H.)
Rachmaninoff—*Etude Tableau*
Rubinstein—*Staccato Etude in C Major*
———— *Etude on False Notes*
Scharwenka—*Staccato Etude in E Flat*
Schumann—*Etudes Symphoniques*
Slozer—Op. 1, No. 2 (Joseffy) (Schirmer)
Smetana—Op. 17. *Am Seegestade*
Sternberg—*Concert Etude in C Minor*
Zarembski—Op. 7. *Etude in G Minor* (Schott)

PIECES IN PERPETUAL MOVEMENT STYLE

Adams, Mrs. Crosby—*Finger Solfeggio* (easy)
Bach, K. P. E.—*Solfeggietto* (A. R. Parson's arr. for left hand alone)
Bartlett, H. N.—Op. 233, No. 2. *The Brook*
———— Op.193, No. 2. *Dragonflies*
Beach, H. H. A.—*The Humming Bird* (Schmidt)
———— *Fireflies*
Beethoven—*Sonata No. 26.* (last movement)
Berge—*La Mouche*
Blumenfeld, F.—Op. 17, No. 23. *Prelude in F*
Brockway, H.—Op. 39, No. 2. *An Idylle of Murmuring Water*
Daquin—*The Cuckoo*
Dubois—*The Enchanted Spring* (from *Poèmes Sylvestres*) (difficult)

———— *Les Myrtilles*
————*Scherzo-Chorale*
Emery, S.—*Fingertwist* (easy)
Gade—Op. 36, No. 4. *Ring Dance* (easy)
Ganschals—*A Forest Brook*
Grutzmacher—Op. 66. *Album Leaf*
Haydn—*Gipsy Rondo*
Heller—Op. 45. No. 1
Hoffmann, H.—Op. 46, No. 3. *Along the Brook* (Schmidt)
Kopilov—*Le Murmure d'un Petit Ruisseau*
Lack—*Le Ruisseau*
Lavalée—*Le Papillon*
Leschetizki—*La Toupie*
MacDowell—*Shadow Dance*
————*Witches' Dance* (difficult)
———— *Elfentanz*
———— *Concert Etude in F Sharp Major*
———— *Czardas*
———— Op. 32. *Scherzino* (double notes) (Schmidt)
Mendelssohn—*Etude in F Major*
———— *Spinning Song C Major* (*Songs Without Words*)
Moszkowski—*Etude in G Major* (*En Automne*)
Mozart—*Sonata No. 7.* (last movement)
Paradies—*Toccata in A*
Pierné—*Cache-cache*
Poldini—*Japanese Etude*
Raff—*La Fileuse*
———— *Toccata* (from *Suite in E Minor*)
Rheinberger—*Ballade in G Minor*
Sapelnikov—Op. 3. *Danse des Elfes*
Schelling—*Un Petit Rien*
Weber—*Perpetual Motion* (also same arr. by Tchaikovsky
for left hand)

PEDAL STUDIES

Blose, Johann—*Pedal Studies* (2 vol.) (Presser)
Gaynor, Jessie L.—*First Pedal Studies* (Presser)
Schytte, L.—*40 Pedal Studies* (Boston Mus. Co.)
Smith, Hannah—*The Pedals*
Venino—*The Pedal* (treatise)

Virgil, Mrs. A. M.—*The Piano Pedals* (The Virgil Piano
    School, New York)
Whiting, Arthur—*Pedal Studies* (2 books)

CONCERT PIECES FOR FOUR HANDS—ONE PIANO
(*Very Easy*)

Alletter—*In Stately Measure*
Bellairs, R.—*Five Finger Studies in Duet Form* (Enoch)
Biedermann—*Dancing Waves*
Chaminade—*Rondeau*
Clementi—*Sonatas* (Universal)
Diabelli—*Easy Exercises* (Universal)
———— Op. 24, 54, 58, 60. *Sonatinas* (Universal)
———— Op. 32, 33, 37. *Sonatas* (Universal)
———— Op. 168. *Pleasures of Youth* (Universal)
———— Op. 150. *Two Sonatas Mignonnes* (Universal)
———— *Rondeau Militaire* (Universal)
Foerster, J. B.—Op. 7. *In the Mountains*
———— Op. 44. *My Youth*
———— Op. 24. *24 Tuneful Exercises* (B. & H.)
———— Op. 97. *For the Young* (B. & H.)
Fuchs—Op. 28. *Easiest Pieces* (Universal)
———— Op. 63. *Andante Grazioso and Capriccio* (Universal)
Grenzbach—*36 Duets on Five Notes* (B. & H.)
Grünfeld—*Little Serenade*
Gurlitt—*24 Preludes and Chorals* (B. & H.)
Sartorio—*Pictures from Youth*
Schmidt, J.—Op. 208, 209. *Sonatinas* (2 books)
Schmidt, Susan—*Easy Tunes for Two* (Schirmer)
Seeboeck—*Six Easy Duets*
———— *Happy Wanderer* (Spanish dance) (Schirmer)
White—*12 Easy Duets*
Willis—*Six Duets*
(*Varying Difficulty*)
Beach, Mrs. H. H. A.—*Summer Dreams*
Beethoven—*Sonata for Four Hands*
———— All overtures and symphonies (Peters)
Bertini—Op. 97. *25 Studies*
Bittner—*Dances from Austria* (Universal)
Bizet—*Menuet de l'Arlésienne in C Minor*

Buzzi-Peccia—*Les Rendezvous (Timide, Galant, Amoureux, Joyeux)*
Chaminade—*Elégie* (from *Album des Enfants*)
———— Op. 53. *Primavera*
———— *La Chaise à Porteurs*
———— *Idylle Arabe*
————*Sérénade d'Automne*
———— *Danse Hindoue*
———— *Rigaudon*
Chopin—Op. 64. *Waltz in D Flat* (arr. by Horn) (Ditson)
————Waltzes, polonaises, nocturnes, mazurkas (complete arr. by Woss) (Universal)
Cui, C.—*Timid Avowal*
Debussy—*Marche Ecossaise* (on a popular tune)
————*Petite Suite (En bateau, Cortège, Menuet, Ballet)* (Durand)
D'Ourville—*Soirées Musicales*
Dutton—*Danse Poétique*
Dvořák—Op. 54. *Waltzes*
Fauré—Op. 10. *Tarentelle*
———— Op. 17. *Three Romances*
————Op. 57. *Shylock (Prélude et Chanson, Madrigal, Nocturne, Final)*
———— Op. 68. *Allegro Symphonique*
————Op. 56. *Dolly (Berceuse, Mia-au, Jardin de Dolly, Kitty, Valse Tendresse, Le Pas Espagnol* (B. M. Co.)
Fischoff—*Ballet Music* (from Schubert's *Rosamunde*)
Fuchs—Op. 48. *Dream Pictures* (Peters)
Gade—Op. 1. *Reminiscenses of Scotland* (B. & H.)
Goldmark, C.—Op. 27. *Ballet Music* (from *Queen of Sheba*) (Pohl, Hamburg)
———— Op. 45. *Scherzo* (Peters)
Grieg—*Pièce Symphonique*
———— Op. 11. *Autumn Overture*
———— *Peer Gynt Suite* (Nos. 1 and 2)
Gurlitt—Op. 147. *Album Leaves*
———— *Spanish Dance*
Hindemith—*Sonata for Four Hands*
Hoffmann, H.—*Leaves from My Journal*
Humperdinck—*Overture to Hänsel und Gretel* (Schott)

Jensen, A.—Op. 43. *Eight Idylls*
————— Op. 45. *Wedding Music*
————— Op. 59. *Evening Music*
————— Op. 60. *Pictures of Life*
————— Op. 62. *Silhouettes*
————— Op. 65. *Rose Bower* and *Dutch Dance*
Jongen—Op. 55. *Pages Intimes* (Chester)
Kuhlau—Op. 46. *Six Sonatas* (Universal)
Liápounov—Op. 16. *Polonaise* (Zimmermann)
MacDowell—Op. 21. *Mondbilder* (Hainauer)
Malipiero—*Pause del Silenzio* (Universal)
Mendelssohn—Overtures and symphonies
Moszkowski—Op. 23. *The Nations* (arr.) (Augener)
————— *Spanish Dances* (arr.)
————— Op. 25. *Deutsche Reigen*
————— Op. 8. *Waltzes* (Peters)
————— Op. 43. *Cortège and Gavotte* (Peters)
————— Op. 51. *Fackeltanz* (Peters)
Mozart—Overtures and symphonies
Nevin, E.—*Country Dance*
Nicode—Op. 29, No.2. *Moorish Dance Song*
Reger, Max—Op. 34. *Cinq Pièces Pittoresques* (Universal)
Ritter, A.—Op. 22. *Olaf's Hochzeitsreigen* (Universal)
Roussel, A.—Op. 39. *Petite Suite* (Durand)
Scharwenka—Op. 21. *Nordisches* (2 books)
————— Op. 38. *Polish Dances* (2 books) (Schirmer)
Schubert—*Impromptu à la Hongroise* (Universal)
Schumann—Op. 66. *Pictures from the East* (Schirmer)
Schütt—Op. 54. *Fairy Tale Waltz* (Universal)
Smith, W.—*Festal Suite*
Södermann—*Swedish Wedding March in F*
Strelezki—*On the Lake of Galilee* (Schirmer)
Suk, J.—Op. 29. *Summer Fairy Tale* (Universal)
Tchaikovsky—*Nutcracker Suite*
—————*Six Symphonies*
Vilm, von—Op. 31. *Nations and Times* (17 pieces in 2 books) (Universal)
————— Op. 70. *Three Characteristic Marches* (Universal)
————— Op. 86. *Waltz Suite* (Universal)
————— Op. 147. *Four Character Pieces* (Universal)

Volkmann—Op. 11. *Musical Picture Book* (Universal)
Vuillemin—*Three Bluettes* (Durand)
Wagner—All operas, marches, etc.

CONCERT PIECES FOR FOUR HANDS—
TWO PIANOS

Aisberg, J.—*Capriccio Hebraique*
Albeniz—*Spanish Rhapsody* (Boston Mus. Co.)
Alnates, E.—Op. 16. *Marche Symphonique* (Hansen)
Anson, Hugo—*The Lone Sailing Ship* (C. Fischer)
Arensky—*Scherzo*
———— Op. 15. *Suite* (Bosworth)
———— Op. 23. *Silhouettes* (Bosworth)
Ashton, A.—*Etudes Symphoniques*
Austen, Thomas—*The Keel Row* (Galaxy Mus. Co.)
Babin, Victor—*Six Etudes* (Universal)
Bach, J. S.—*Concert in F* (Steingraber)
———— *Fugue for Two Pianos* (Peters)
———— *Concert in C Major* (Peters)
Bach-Bauer—*Prelude and Fugue in C Minor* (Ditson)
———— *Fantasie and Fugue in A Minor* (Ditson)
———— *Concerto in C Minor* (Schirmer)
Bach-Foss—*See What His Love Can Do* (C. Fischer)
Bach-Gest—*Choral* (*Jesu Bleibt Meine Freude*) (Schirmer)
Bach-Gobbi—*Organ Fugue in A Minor* (Roszarlgyi)
Bach-Howe—*Jesu, Der Du Meine Seele* (Galaxy Mus. Co.)
———— *It Is a True Saying* (C. Fischer)
———— *Wir Eilen* (C. Fischer)
————*Schafe Können Sicher Weiden* (C. Fischer)
Bach-Keller—*Organ Passacaglia in C Minor* (Ditson)
Bach-Lee—*Four Dance Measures* (C. Fischer)
Bach-Le Fleming—*Two Chorales* (Chester)
———— *Mortify Us by Thy Grace* (*Cantata 22*)
———— *Jesu, Source of Our Desire* (*Cantata 147*)
Bach-Maier—*Sicilienne* (J. Fischer)
———— *Five 2 Part Inventions* (J. Fischer)
Bach-Reger-Pillney—*Variations and Fugue* (Am. Mus. Pub.)
Bach-Rheinberger—*Air with Thirty Variations* (Kistner)
Bach-Ross—*Gigue in C* (C. Fischer)

Bach-Scott—*Jig Fugue* (C. Fischer)
Bach-Siloti—*Andante* (*Brandenburg Concerto* III) (C. Fischer)
———— *Andante* (*Concert for Two Pianos*) (C. Fischer)
Bach-Tate—*Sarabande in E Minor* (*English Suite*) (C. Fischer)
———— *March, Sarabande, Polonaise* (C. Fischer)
Bach-Towsey—*Organ Prelude and Toccata D Minor* (C. Fischer)
Bach-Whitaker—*Wachet Auf* (C. Fischer)
Bach-Williams—*Suite* (*Gavotte, Minuet, Fugue*) (C. Fischer)
Bach-Wilson—*Adagio* (*Brandenburg Concerto* VI) (C. Fischer)
Bach, Wm. F.—*Sonata for Two Pianos* (Boston Mus. Co.)
Bax, A.—*Moy Mell*
Beach, Mrs. H. H. A.—*Suite on Irish Melodies*
Beethoven-Liszt—*Ruins of Athens Fantasie*
Beethoven-Thern—*Turkish March*
Behr, Franz—Op. 443. *Mitzi-Kätzchen* (Doblinger)
Berkley, L.—*Capriccio*
———— *Nocturne*
———— *Polka*
Berlioz-Hutcheson—*Rakoczy March* (J. Fischer)
Boyle—*Concerto in D Minor* (Schirmer)
Brahms—Op. 23. *Variations on a Theme by Schumann* (Rieter-Biedermann)
———— *Hungarian Dances*
———— Op. 56. *Variations on a Theme by Haydn*
———— *Quintet in F Minor*
Brahms-Hughes—Op. 39. *Waltzes* (Schirmer)
Brahms-Kramer—*4 Choral Preludes* (J. Fischer)
Brahms-Maier—*12 Liebeslieder* (Sets 1 and 2) (J. Fischer)
———— *Six Waltzes* (Schirmer)
Brand-Vrabely—*Concert Piece in Hungarian Style* (Doblinger)
Braun, R.—*Divertimento* (B. & H.)
Bruhl, Ignaz—Op. 6. *Tarantella*
———— Op. 64. *Theme and Variations*
———— *Pastorale*
———— *In Arabian Style*

———— Op. 65. *Rhapsody* (arr. by author)
Busoni, F.—*Duettino Concertante* (B. & H.)
Carnevali, V.—*A Naïad's Dream* (J. Fischer)
Chaminade, C.—Op. 36. *Intermède* (Costallat)
———— *Concert Piece*
———— *Andante and Scherzettino* (Costallat)
———— Op. 79. *Le Matin* (Costallat)
———— Op. 59. *Le Soir* (Costallat)
———— Op. 73. *Valse Carnavalesque* (Enoch)
Chasins, A.—*Künstlerleben* (Strauss) (J. Fischer)
———— *The Blue Danube* (Strauss) (J. Fischer)
———— *Melodie* from *Orpheus* (Gluck) (C. Fischer)
Chopin-Gould-Shefter—*Fantasie Impromptu* (C. Fischer)
Chopin-Hesselburg—Op. 78. *Rondo in C* (J. Church)
———— Op. 10. *Etudes* (J. Church)
———— Op. 25, Nos. 1 and 2, *Etudes* (J. Church)
Chopin-Maier—*Etude in F Minor* (J. Fischer)
Chopin-Miller—Op. 64. *Waltz in D Flat* (J. Fischer)
Chopin-Nicode—*Allegro de Concert* (Augener)
Chopin-Scharwenka—*Scherzo in B Flat Minor* (B. & H.)
Clementi, M.—*Sonata* (B. & H.)
Clementi-Thimm—Op. 36. *Six Sonatas* (easy)
Converse, F.—*Night and Day* (Schirmer)
———— *Two Etudes in G Flat* (J. Fischer)
Couperin—*Le Letville* (C. Fischer)
Couperin-Prosniz—*Allemande* (Doblinger)
Debussy—*In White and Black*
———— *Images* (Bos. Mus. Co.)
D'Erlanger, F.—*Midnight Roses* (Hansen)
Dóhnanyi—*Wedding Waltz* from *The Veil of Pierrette* (Doblinger)
Dunhill, T.—*Two Pastorales* (C. Fischer)
Duvernoy—Op. 256. *Feu Roulant* (Augener)
Dvorak—*Slavic Dance in C, No. 1*
Farnaby, G.—*For Two Virginals* (C. Fischer)
Fauré, G.—Op. 62. *Valse Caprice in A Flat* (Bos. Mus. Co.)
———— Op. 19. *Ballade* (Bos. Mus. Co.)
Fischhof, R.—*Trois Scènes Aragonaises* (Doblinger)
Friedman, I.—Op. 70. *Suite* (Hansen)
Gaillard, M.—*Images d'Epinal* (Hansen)
Glass, L.—Op. 47. *Fantasie* (Hansen)

Gliere—*Danse Populaire*
Gluck-Chasins—*Melodie* from *Orpheus* (2nd ballet) (C.
Fischer)
Gobbi—*Scherzo* from *Midsummer Night's Dream* (Ros-
zarolgyi)
———— *Organ Fugue in A Minor* (Bach) (Roszarolgyi)
————*Scherzo* (Mendelssohn) (Roszarolgyi)
———— *Novellette in D* (Schumann) (Roszarolgyi)
Godard, B.—Op. 49. *Introduction and Allegro* (Durand)
Gould, Morton—*Rumbolero* (C. Fischer)
Grainger, P.—*Hill Songs, 1 and 2, Children's March, In a
Nutshell* (Schirmer)
———— *Eastern Intermezzo* (Schirmer)
Grieg—Op. 51. *Romanza with Variations* (Peters)
Grieg-Kronke—Op. 19. *On the Mountains* (Church)
Grieg-Saar—Op. 43. *The Butterfly* (Church)
Grieg-Werthner—*Peer Gynt Suite, No. 2* (Church)
Haigh, A. C.—*Bourrée d'Auvergne* (J. Fischer)
———— *Winter, Nightfall, Lake of Innisfree* (J. Fischer)
Hassler, J. W.—*Gigue in D Minor* (Steingraber)
Heller, S.—Op. 85, No. 2. *Tarentelle* (B. & H.)
Henselt-Maier—*Etude in F Minor* (J. Fischer)
Herzogenberg—Op. 13. *Theme and Variations* (Doblinger)
Hesselberg—*El Trocadero* (Church)
Hollander, A.—Op. 61. *Variations on a Schubert Theme*
(Universal)
———— Op. 64. *Eight Landlers in Triple Time* (Universal)
———— *Perpetual Motion* (Weber) (Schirmer)
Howell, D.—*Mazurka* (C. Fischer)
Ireland, John—*Concerto in E Flat* (arr. by author) (Chester)
Kelberine, A.—*Londonderry Air* (G. Schirmer)
Kirchner—Op. 86. *Waltzes* (Peters)
Knorr—Op. 8. *Russian Song* (B. & H.)
Kowalski-Jonas—*Marche Hongroise* (C. Fischer)
Krause—Op. 17. *Sonata in E* (B. & H.)
Kronke, Emil—*Symphonische Variationen* (Steingraber)
Liszt—*Les Préludes*
———— *Concert for Two Pianos* (no orchestra) (B. & H.)
———— *Hungarian Fantasie* (Schirmer)
———— *Fantasie on Ruins of Athens* (Beethoven)
Marx, K.—*Castelli Romani* (Hansen)

Mason, D. G.—Op. 226. *Scherzo* (C. Fischer)
———— *Prelude and Fugue* (J. Fischer)
Mathews, H. A.—*The Pines* (Ditson)
Melan-Gueroult—Op. 7. *Scherzo* (Costallat)
Mendelssohn—*Rondo in E Flat* (Peters)
———— Op. 32. *Capriccio Brillante* (Peters)
Mendelssohn-Sutro—*Elfin Dance* (Church)
———— *Entrance of the Clowns*
———— *Nocturne*
———— *Dance of the Clowns*
———— Op. 16. *Scherzo*
Menter, Sophie—*Hungarian Gipsy Style* (Schirmer)
Merikanto, O.—*Menuetto* (Schroder & Gunther)
Messner, J.—*Symphonietta* (Doblinger)
Miller, J.—*South of the Rio Grande* (J. Fischer)
Monti-Gould—*Czardas* (C. Fischer)
Moscheles, I.—Op. 92. *Homage à Handel* (Augener)
Moszkowski-Silver—*Valse Brillante in A Flat* (J. Fischer)
Moussorgsky-Hesselberg—*Hopak* (Summy)
Mozart—*Sonata in D* (Steingraber)
———— *Concerto in E Flat* (with cadenzas) (Steingraber)
Mozart-Grieg—*Sonatas* (in F major, C minor, C major and
        G major) (second piano part by Grieg) (Peters)
Mozart-Maier—*Allegro* (*Quasi Carillon*) (C. Fischer)
———— *Menuet* (C. Fischer)
———— *Andante and Menuet* (C. Fischer)
———— *Allegro* (sonatina for violin and piano in C minor)
        (C. Fischer)
Mozart-Reinecke—*Concert Allegro* (Leukart)
Mozart-Rheinberger—*Variations* (Leukart)
Mozart-Wagner, J.—*Lodron Concerto* (Schirmer)
Mozart-Wilson—*Romance* (*Kleine Nachtmusik*) (C. Fisch-
        er)
Nollet-Hesselberg—*Elegy* (Summy)
Parrish, Carl—*Valse Viennoise* (J. Fischer)
Pasquini-Boghen—*Two Sonatas* (Durand)
Pasquini-Reichel—*Caprice in E* (Ries & Erler, Berlin)
Poldini-Hesselberg—*The House of Cards* (C. Fischer)
———— *The King, Queen of Hearts, Dance of the Jack*
Powell, J. A.—*Natchez on the Hill* (3 Virginia country
        dances) (Schirmer)

Rachmaninoff—*First Suite*
———— Op. 17. *Second Suite* (Gutheil)
———— Op. 5. *Fantasie* (Gutheil)
Rachmaninoff-Hesselberg—Op. 28, No. 5. *Prelude Militaire* (Summy)
———— *Prelude in C Sharp Minor*
Raff—Op. 200, No. 2. *Gavotte and Musette in C Sharp Minor* (Kistner)
Reger-Pillney—*Variations and Fugue on a Bach Theme* (A. M. P.)
Reinecke, C.—*Gondoliera* (easy) (Ditson)
———— *Improvisation on a Gavotte by Gluck*
———— *Improvisation on a Theme from Manfred* (Schumann)
———— Op. 94. *La Belle Griselidis*
———— *Concert Allegro* (Mozart) (Leukart)
Rheinhold—Op. 7. *Suite for Piano and String Orchestra* (Kistner)
Rimski-Korsakov-Enders—*Flight of the Bumblebee* (Schirmer)
Ropartz, Guy de—*Pièce en Si Mineur*
Saar, V. L.—*Gavotte Intermezzo* (C. Fischer)
Saint-Saëns, C.—Op. 65. *Menuet and Gavotte from Septet* (Durand)
———— Op. 96. *Caprice Arabe*
———— Op. 87. *Scherzo* (original)
———— *Variations on a Theme by Beethoven* (original)
———— *Suite Algérienne* (arr. by Saint-Saëns) (Durand)
———— *Rouet d'Omphale*
————*Marche Héroique*
Sauer, Emil—*Boîte à Musique*
Scharwenka—Op. 32. *Scherzo from Concerto in B Flat Minor* (arr. by author) (Schirmer)
Schennich, Emil—*Fantasia Estatica* (Doblinger)
Schmidt, Hans.—Op. 62. *Emperor Etude* (Doblinger)
Scholz, R.—*Prelude, Choral, Fughetto and Toccata* (Schirmer)
Schubert-Bauer—Op. 84. *Rondo Brillante, No. 2* (Schirmer)
Schubert-Horwath—*Marche Militaire* (Steingraber)
Schubert-Liszt-Hesselberg—*Erl King* (Summy)
Schubert-Winding—Op. 84. *Theme and Variations* (Hansen)

Schubert-Zellner—*Rosamunde Overture* (Spina)
Schultz—*Rondos* (in G major, F major, and A minor)
Schumann, R.—Op. 46. *Andante and Variations* (Pohl)
Schumann-Maier—*Scherzo from E Flat Quartet* (J. Fischer)
Schumann-Mohn—*Rondo Brillante* (Bote & Bock)
Schütt, E.—Op. 9. *Variations on an Original Theme* (Aug. Cranz)
———— *Valse Paraphrase*
Scionti, Silvio—*Star-Spangled Banner* (J. S. Smith) (Ditson)
Seeboeck, W. C.—*Menuel al Antico* (Church)
Sinding, Chris.—Op. 2. *Variations in E Flat Minor* (Hansen)
———— Op. 41. *Andante*
———— *Deciso ma non troppo allegro* (Hansen)
Somervell, Arthur—*Variations on Original Theme* (Augener)
Spross, Gil.—*Valse Caprice* (Presser)
Taylor, Deems—*Through the Looking Glass Suite* (J. Fischer)
Tchaikovsky-Horvath—Op. 2, No. 3. *Song Without Words* (Steingraber)
Tchaikovsky-Ludwig—*Troika Ride* (Forberg)
Tchaikovsky-Schaefer—*Barcarolle*
Thompson, Roy—*Aubade* (C. Fischer)
Turner, Olive—*Cap and Bells* (C. Fischer)
———— *Two Cornish Sketches* (C. Fischer)
Vogt—Op. 18. *Prelude and Fugue*
Von Wilm—Op. 72. *Waltz* (Leukart)
———— Op. 64. *Variations* (Leukart)
Wachtmeister—*Prelude and Fugue* (Church)
Wagner-Ehrlich—*Walkürenritt* (Schott)
———— *Song of the Rhine Nymphs* (Schott)
———— *Siegfried's Funeral March* (Schott)
Walton-Seiber—*Popular Song (Façade)* (C. Fischer)
Weber-Corder—*Invitation to the Dance* (Bosworth)
Weinberger—*Schwanda Polka* (arr. by author) (Ass. Mus. Pub.)
Welleba, L.—Op. 1. *Concert Waltz* (Doblinger)
Zellner—Op. 16. *Duet on Motives from Melunia* (Doblinger)
Zipoli-Anderson-Scionti—*Prelude and Fugue* (J. Fischer)
————48 *Pieces for Two Pianos, Four Hands* (Harcourt, Brace & Co.)

CONCERT PIECES FOR SIX HANDS—
TWO PIANOS

Bach—Op. 70. *Divertissement*
Beethoven—*Siegesmarsch aus König Stephan* (Brauer)
———— *Overture* to *Egmont*
Czerny—Op. 609. *Les Trois Soeurs*
————*Les Pianistes Associés* (Books 1 to 14) (Spina)
Ferd, Friedrich—Op. 333. *Die Drei Schwestern*
Grainger, P.—*Green Bushes* (Passacaglia) (Schirmer)
———— *English Dance* (2 copies necessary) (Schirmer)
———— *Country Gardens* (Schirmer)
Gurlitt—Op. 192. (2 books—6 Tonstücke)
Krug—Op. 349. *Les Trois Amies*
Mozart-Burchard—*Overture* to *The Magic Flute* (Brauer)
Rheinberger—Op. 94. *Concerto in A Flat* (Schott)
Rummel—Op. 66. *Rondo in Form of a Waltz* (Schott)

CONCERT PIECE FOR SIX HANDS—ONE PIANO

Grainger, Percy—*Zanzibar Boat Song* (Schirmer)

CONCERT PIECES FOR EIGHT HANDS—TWO PIANOS

Beethoven—Op. 20. *Septet* (Augener)
Beethoven-Parlow—*Country Dances*
Bizet-Kronke—*Scherzo* from *Roma* (Steingraber)
Brahms—*Hungarian Dances*
Gurlitt—*Rustic Pictures* (3 books) (Augener)
Jensen-Kronke—Op. 45. *Wedding Music* (Steingraber)
Mendelssohn—*Wedding March*
———— *Nocturne*
———— Op. 20. *Octet in E Flat*
Mohr, A.—Op. 29. *Sonatine, March, Rondo, and Allegro*
Moszkowski—*Valse Brillante*
Scharwenka—*Polish Dances* (Augener)
Schubert—*Six Celebrated Marches* (Augener)
Schubert-Kronke—*Soirée de Vienne, Nos. 2 and 4* (Steingraber)
Schubert-Parlow—*Children's March*
Wagner-Debrosse—*Meistersinger Overture* (Schott)

Weber-Kronke—*Invitation to the Dance* (Steingraber)
Wolff, B.—Op. 21. *Menuet*
Zipold—Op. 13. *Konzertstück*

CONCERT PIECES FOR PIANO AND ORGAN

Clokey, J.—*Symphonic Pieces* (*Dialogue, Romance, Scherzo, Intermezzo, Fugue*) (J. Fischer)
Demarest, Clifford—*Fantasie* (Schirmer)
———— *Grand Aria* (Schirmer)
———— *Rhapsody* (Schirmer)
Dupré, M.—*Ballade* (Gray)
Franck, C.—*Prelude, Fugue and Variation* (Durand)
————*Pièce Héroique* (arr. by Harold Schwab) (Gray)
Grasse, E.—*Festival Overture in D* (2 copies needed) (Schirmer)
Karg-Elert—*Harmonium and Piano* (Simon, Berlin)
———— Op. 22, 1, 4, 6, 7
———— Op. 29, *7 Silhouettes*
———— Op. 35, *5 Poesien*
Kroeger, Ernest—Op. 94. *Nocturne* (J. Fischer)
Mason, D. G.—*Prelude and Fugue* (J. Fischer)
Saint-Saëns—Op. 8. *Fantasy and Fugue, Choral, Scherzo, Finale* (Froment)
Sowerby, Leo—*Mediaeval Poem* (Gray)
Stoughton, R. S.—*Dreams* (White, Smith & Co.)
True, Latham—*In a Gothic Cathedral* (J. Fischer)
———— *Moonlight on a Pagan Temple* (J. Fischer)
Yon, P.—*Concerto Gregoriano* (J. Fischer)
Wagner-Karg-Elert—*Two Books of Arrangements* (*Parsifal, Lohengrin, Tannhäuser, etc.*) (Peters)

SONATAS FOR PIANO AND VIOLIN

Beethoven—Op. 24. *Sonata in F Major* (Springtime)
———— Op. 30. *Sonata in E Flat*
———— Op. 30. *Sonata in G Major*
———— Op. 47. (*Kreutzer Sonata*)
———— Op. 62. *Sonata in D Major*
Brahms—Op. 57. *Sonata 1 in G Major*
———— Op. 100. *Sonata 2 in A Major*

—— Op. 108. *Sonata 3 in C Minor*
Dvořák—Op. 57. *Sonata*
—— Op. 100. *Sonatine*
Fauré, G.—Op. 73. *Sonata in A Major* (B. & H.)
Franck, C.—*Sonata* (difficult)
Fuchs, R.—Op. 77. *Sonata in E Flat* (Universal)
Gade—Op. 6. *Sonata 1*
—— Op. 21. *Sonata 2*
—— Op. 59. *Sonata 3*
—— Op. 8. *Sonata 1 in F* (Peters)
—— Op. 13. *Sonata 2 in G Minor* (Peters)
—— Op. 45. *Sonata 3 in C Minor* (Peters)
Handel—*Sonata 3 in A*
—— *Sonata 10 in G Minor*
—— *Sonata 12 in F*
—— *Sonata 13 in D*
—— *Sonata 15 in E*
Haydn—*Sonata No. 6 in C*
—— *Sonata No. 8 in G*
Lazzari—Op. 24. *Sonata* (Durand)
Melville, M.—Op. 6. *Sonata in G Major* (Simrock)
Moor, E.—Op. 54. *Sonata* (Mathot)
Mozart—*Sonatas in E Flat, E Minor, F Major, and B Flat*
Paderewski—Op. 13. *Sonata* (B. & B.)
Pierné, G.—Op. 36. *Sonata* (Durand)
Porpora—*Sonata in G Major* (B. & H.)
Pugnani—*Sonata*
Rubinstein, A. Op. 13. *Sonata in G*
—— Op. 19. *Sonata in A Minor*
Rust—*Sonata in D Minor* (Peters)
Sachs, Leo.—*Sonata* (Mathot)
Saint-Saëns, C.—*Sonata No. 1* (Durand)
—— Op. 102. *Sonata No. 2*
—— Op. 162. *Sonata No. 3*
Scalero, R.—Op. 12. *Sonata* (B. & H.)
Schumann, G.—Op. 12. *Sonata* (Leukart)
Schumann, R.—Op. 105. *Three Sonatas* (Peters)
Sinding—Op. 47. *Sonata*
—— *Sonata No. 1 in C Major*
—— Op. 99. *Sonata in D Minor*
Sjogren—Op. 24. *Sonata in E Minor*

Smith, D. S.—*Sonata* (Schirmer)
Strauss, R.—Op. 18. *Sonata in E Flat*
Terry, Frances—*Sonata* (Schirmer)
Wagenaar, B.—*Sonata* (Schirmer)

CONCERT PIECES FOR PIANO AND TWO VIOLINS

Arensky-Borch—Op. 30. *Serenade* (C. Fischer)
Bach, J. S.—*Sonata in C Minor*
———— *2 Sonatas* (David) *in C and G* (B. & H.)
———— *Concerto in D Minor* (B. & H.)
Bach-Hinze-Reinhold—*Sonata in G* (A. M. P.)
Beriot, C. de—Op. 57. *Three Duos Concertants* (Schirmer)
Boyce—*Sonata in A* (Augener)
Corelli—*Sarabande in B Flat*
Corelli-Klengel—*Two Chamber Sonatas*
Corelli-Sitt—Op. 4. *Six Chamber Sonatas*
Couperin—*Le Parnasse* (Durand)
Godard, B.—Op. 18. *Six Duets* (Schott)
Handel—*Nine Sonatas* (cello ad. lib.)
———— *Six Sonatas* (Krause)
Handke, R.—Op. 23. *Rondoletto* (B. & H.)
Juon, P.—Op. 9. *Silhouetten* (Books I and II) (Schlesinger)
———— Op. 43. *Silhouetten* (Books III and IV) (Schlesinger)
———— Op. 81. *Seven Little Tone Poems* (Schlesinger)
Manen, J.—*Jurentus* (2 violins, 2 pianos, 4 hands) (Universal)
Mendelssohn, Arnold—*Trio in A minor* (pianos, 2 violins)
Molique—*Concertante* (B. & H.)
Moszkowski—Op. 71. *Suite* (Peters)
Mozart—*Concertone in C* (B. & H.)
Pleyel, I.—Op. 8. *Six Duets* (Schirmer)
———— Op. 48. *Six Duets* (easy)
———— Op. 59. *Six Duets*
Porpora—*Four Sonatas* (Laccetti) (Curei, Naples)
Purcell—*The Golden Sonata* (Augener)
———— *Sonatas* (in B minor, A minor, C major) (Augener)
Sinding—Op. 56. *First Serenade* (Hansen)
———— Op. 92. *Second Serenade* (Peters)
Stoessel, A.—*Suite Antique* (Schirmer)
———— *Sonata for Two Violins and Piano* (Schirmer)

Torelli—Op. 8. *Concerto* (Augener)
Veracini—*Sonata in C Minor* (B. & H.)
Vivaldi-Nachez—*Concerto in A Minor* (Schott)
Wieniawski—Op. 18. *Eight Caprices* (no piano) (Schirmer)

SONATAS FOR PIANO AND CELLO

Bach, J. S.—*Sonatas* (Van Lier) (Universal)
Bach, K. P. E.—*Three Sonatas* (B. & H.)
Beethoven—*Five Sonatas* (Peters)
Bennett, W. S.—Op. 32. *Sonata* (Augener)
Berghout—Op. 34. *Sonatine* (Augener)
Bernard, E.—Op. 46. *Sonata in G* (Durand)
Boellmann, L.—Op. 40. *Sonata* (Durand)
——— *Symphonic Variations*
Brahms—Op. 38. *Sonata in E Minor* (Universal)
Chevillard—Op. 15. *Sonata* (Durand)
Chopin—Op. 65. *Sonata* (B. & H.)
Fauré, G.—*Papillon* (Hamelle)
——— *Sicilienne* (Hamelle)
——— *Elégie* (Hamelle)
Foerster, J. B.—Op. 45. *Sonata* (Universal)
Geminiani—*Sonata in C Minor* (B. & H.)
Giorni, A.—*Sonata* (Schirmer)
Godard—Op. 104. *Sonata D Minor* (Durand)
Gretchaninov—Op. 113. *Sonata* (Schott)
Grieg—Op. 36. *Sonata in A Minor* (Peters)
Handel—*Sonata in G Major* (Augener)
——— *Sonatas* (in A minor, G major, F major) (Schott)
Herzogenberg—*Sonata in E Flat Major*
Hure, J.—*Sonata 1903*
——— *Sonata 1906*
Jemain—*Sonata* (Durand)
Jensen, G.—Op. 26. *Sonata in A Minor* (Augener)
Juon, P.—Op. 34. *Sonata* (Schlesinger)
Klengel, J.—Op. 48. *Three Sonatas* (in C minor, D, and E
        minor) (B. & H.)
——— Op. 47. *Three Sonatas* (in C, A minor, and G)
        (B. & H.)
Kogler—*Sonata in F Major*
Kornaught—*Sonata in E Minor*

Kuhnel—*Sonata in A*
Lazarus—Op. 56. *Sonata in D Minor* (Universal)
Marcello—*Two Sonatas* (Piatti) (Universal)
Mendelssohn—Op. 45. *Sonata* (Universal)
———— Op. 58. *Sonata*
Moor, E.—Op. 76. *Sonata* (Mathot)
Nicode—Op. 23. *Sonata in B Major* (B. & H.)
Pfitzner—Op. 1. *Sonata in F Sharp Minor* (B. & H.)
Rachmaninoff—Op. 19. *Sonata* (Gutheil)
Ropartz, G. de—*Sonata* (Durand)
Rubinstein, A.—*Three Sonatas* (Op. 18, in D, Op. 39, and
     Op. 49) (Universal)
Saint-Saëns, C.—*Two Sonatas* (Op. 32, in C minor and Op.
     123) (Durand)
Scharwenka,—Op. 46. *Sonata in E Minor* (Augener)
Strauss, R.—Op. 6. *Sonata in F Major* (Universal)
Von Wilm—Op. 111. *Sonata in A Minor* (Universal)
Windesperger—Op. 11. *Sonata for Cello and Organ* (Schott)
Wolfrum—Op. 7. *Sonata in E Minor* (Universal)

CONCERT PIECES FOR PIANO AND VIOLA

Alard—*Classical Masters* (Schott)
Ariosti—*Six Sonatas* (Piatti) (Schott)
Bach, J. S.—*Three Sonatas* (B. & H.)
Beethoven—*Romanzas* (Peters)
Bowen, Y.—*Two Sonatas* (C minor and F major) (Schott)
Bruch—Op. 55. *Canzona* (B. & H.)
———— Op. 85. *Romanza* (Schott)
Cools, E.—*Poème* (A.M.P.)
———— *Andante Serio* (A.M.P.)
Goltermann—Op. 15. *Duet* (Augener)
———— Op. 25. *Duet* (Augener)
———— Op. 114. *Sonatina* (Augener)
Grazioli—*Sonata in F*
Handel—*Sonata di Gamba* (arr. by Jensen)
———— *Sonata in B* (Alard) (Schott)
Herrmann—Op. 27. *Notturno rimesso* (Augener)
Herzogenberg—*Legends* (Universal)
Joachim, J.—Op. 9. *Hebrew Melodies* (B. & H.)
———— Op. 10. *Variations* (B. & H.)
Juon, P.—Op. 15. *Sonata* (Schlesinger)

Kalliwoda—*Six Nocturnes* (Peters)
Klengel, P.—Op. 39. *Six Pieces* (B. & H.)
Krenz—Op. 20. *Concerto* (Augener)
———— Op. 45. *Suite* (Augener)
Marcello—*Sonata in E Minor*
Mozart—*Two Duos* (viola and violin) (Universal)
Prout—Op. 26. *Sonata in D Major*
Raff, J.—Op. 85. *Six Morceaux*
Ritter, T.—*Tone Piece*
Rubinstein, A.—Op. 11. *Three Salon Pieces* (Augener)
———— Op. 49. *Sonata in F Minor* (B. & H.)
Schumann, R.—Op. 94. *Three Romanzas*
———— Op. 102. *Five Pieces im Folkston*
———— Op. 113. *Märchenbilder*
Sitt, Hans—Op. 39. *Albumleaves* (Peters)
Steiner—Op. 44. *Concerto* (Universal)
Strauss, R. *At a Lonely Fount* (Universal)
Thomas, E.—*Sonatine in C* (Augener)
Vieuxtemps—Op. 30. *Elegy* (Augener)
Walker—*Sonata in C* (Schott)

PIANO TRIOS
(PIANO, VIOLIN AND CELLO UNLESS OTHERWISE NOTED)

Arensky—Op. 32. *Trio in D Minor* (Jurgensen)
Bax, A.—*Trio in one Movement* (violin and viola) (Chester)
Beethoven—*Ten Trios* (Op. 1, No. 3; Op. 70, No. 1; Op. 97, in B flat are the best)
Brahms—Op. 8. *Trio in B Major* (superb) (Universal)
———— Op. 40. *Trio in E Flat* (violin and French horn) (Universal)
———— Op. 87. *Trio in C Major* (Universal)
———— Op. 101. *Trio in C Minor* (Universal)
———— Op. 114. *Trio in A Minor* (clarinet and cello) (Universal)
Chaminade—Op. 34. *Trio in A Minor* (Costallat)
D'Indy, V.—Op. 29. *Trio in E Flat* (piano, clarinet and cello) (Hamelle)
Dvořák—Op. 90. *Dumky Trio* (Universal)
Fenney, W.—Op. 20. *Trio in G Major* (Chester)
Gade—Op. 29. *Novelletten* (very useful)

———— Op. 42. *Trio in F* (good)

Godard—Op. 72. *Trio in F Major* (Durand)

Goossens—Op. 7. *Five Impressions of a Holiday* (harp or piano, flute and violin) (Chester)

Gurlitt—Op. 129—*Easy Trio* (Augener)

————Op. 171. *Easy Trio* (Augener)

———— Op. 181. *Miniature Trio* (Augener)

Haydn—*Thirty-one Trios* (7, 17, 19, 30 are best) (B. & H.)

Hennessy—Op. 10. *Three Short Easy Trios*

Jadassohn—Op. 85. *Trio in C Minor* (B. & H.)

Jensen, G.—Op. 27. *Fantasiestücke* (violin and viola) (Augener)

Jongen, J.—*Trio* (violin, viola, and piano)

Juon, P.—Op. 19, No. 2. *Barkarole* (Schlesinger)

———— Op. 39. *Trio Caprice* (Goesta Berling) (Schlesinger)

———— Op. 9. *Silhouetten* (violin, viola, and piano) (Schlesinger)

———— Op. 43. *Silhouetten* (violin, viola, and piano) (Schlesinger)

Klengel—Op. 35. *Two Trios for Children in C and G* (B. & H.)

Kreuz, E.—Op. 31. *Easy Trio*

Lacombe—Op. 12. *Trio in G Major* (B. & H.)

Leclair—*Sonata 8 in D* (violin and flute, or viola and cello) (B. & H.)

Malipiero—*Sonata a tre* (piano, violin, and cello) (A.M.P.)

Mason, D. G.—*Pastorale* (violin and clarinet) (Schirmer)

Mendelssohn—*Duetto* (*Song Without Words*)

———— Op. 49. *Trio No. 1 in D Minor*

———— Op. 66. *Trio No. 2 in C Minor*

Meyer—Op. 8. *Three Trios for Children*

Moor, E.—Op. 81. *Trio* (piano, violin, and cello) (Mathot)

Mozart—*Eight Trios* (B and G are the nicest)

Napravnik—Op. 24. *Trio in G Minor*

Navratil, K.—Op. 9. *Trio*

Pierné, G.—Op. 45. *Trio in C Minor* (Durand)

Purcell—*The Golden Sonata* (piano and 2 violins) (Augener)

Rachmaninoff—Op. 9. *Trio in Memory of the Cellist Davidoff* (difficult, fine)

Rameau—*Pièces en Concert* (piano, violin and cello or piano, flute and cello) (Durand)

Reinecke—Op. 126. *Two Serenades* (Easy)

Reissiger—Op. 181. *Trio in G Minor* (Universal)
——— Op. 85. *Trio*
——— Op. 97. *Trio*
Rheinberger—Op. 121. *Trio Suite* (organ, violin and cello)
(Torberg)
——— Op. 112. *Trio No. 2*
——— Op. 121. *Trio No. 3*
Rubinstein—Op. 15. *Two Trios* (F major and G minor)
——— Op. 52. *Trio in B Flat Major*
——— Op. 85. *Trio in A Minor*
Saint George—*First Petite Suite* (Augener)
Saint-Saëns—Op. 18. *Trio in F Major*
——— Op. 92. *Trio in E Minor*
Scharwenka—Op. 45. *Trio in A Minor* (B & H.)
——— Op. 105. *Trio* (B. & H.)
Schubert—Op. 99. *Trio in B Flat Major*
——— Op. 100. *Trio in E Flat*
Schumann, G.—Op. 25. *Trio in F* (Leukart)
Schumann, R.—Op. 32—*Märchen-Erzählungen* (violin and
clarinet or viola) (Litolff)
——— Op. 88. *Fantasiestücke* (moderately difficult) (Peters)
——— Op. 63. *Trio No. 1 in D Minor* (Peters)
——— Op. 80. *Trio No. 2 in F Major* (Peters)
——— Op. 110. *Trio No. 3 in G Minor* (Peters)
Schütt—Op. 27. *Trio in C Minor*
——— Op. 72. *Episoden* (Simrock)
——— Op. 51. *Trio in E Minor* (Simrock)
——— Op. 54. *Walzermärchen* (Universal)
Smetana—Op. 15. *Trio in G Minor*
Soething—Op. 36. (3 vols.) (easy) (Universal)
Tchaikovsky—Op. 50. *Trio* (in memory of Nicolas Rubin-
stein) (superb, difficult)
Volkmann—Op. 5. *Trio in B Flat Minor* (B. & H.)
Weber—Op. 63. *Trio in C Minor* (Peters)

PIANO QUARTETS
(VIOLIN, VIOLA AND CELLO WITH PIANO
UNLESS OTHERWISE NOTED)

Beethoven—*Sonata Movements* (3 books) (easy) (Augener)
——— No. 1, in E flat major (Universal)
——— No. 2, in E major

—————— No. 3, in C major
—————— No. 4, in E flat major
Berghout—Op. 42 (Steingraber)
Brahms—Op. 25, in G major (Universal)
—————— Op. 26, in A major
—————— Op. 60, in C minor
Bungert—Op. 18
Chausson—Op. 30 (fine)
Dall'Abaco—Op. 3. *Four Trio Sonatas* (2 violins, cello, bass, and piano) (B. & H.)
Dvořák—Op. 87, in E flat (Simrock)
—————— Op. 47 (2 violins, cello, and piano or organ) (Universal)
Fauré, G.—Op. 15, No. 1 (Hamelle)
Foote, A.—Op. 23, in C major
Fuchs, R.—Op. 75, in B minor
Gernsheim—Op. 6, in E flat
Goetz—Op. 6, in E flat major (B. & H.)
Gounod—Op. 35, in B minor
Hermann, H.—Op. 55, in B flat (Steingraber)
Hoffmann, H.—Op. 50, in D minor
Jadassohn—Op. 77, in C minor
Jensen, G. Op. 27. *Fantasiestücke* (violins, viola) (Augener)
Jongen, J.—Op. 23 (beautiful) (Durand)
Juon—Op. 37. *Rhapsody in F Major*
—————— Op. 50. *Quartet* (Schlesinger)
—————— Op. 29. *Quartet* (Schlesinger)
Kiel—Op. 43, in A minor
—————— Op. 44, in E major
—————— Op. 50, in G major
Krug, Arnold—Op. 16, in C minor
Labor—Op. 6, in C major
Lekeu, W.—*Quartet in B Minor* (unfinished) (Rouart)
Marx—*Rhapsody* (Universal)
—————— *Ballade* (Universal)
—————— *Scherzo* (Universal)
Mendelssohn—Op. 3, in B minor (Universal)
Mozart—No. 1, in G minor (Peters)
—————— No. 2, in E flat major (Peters)
—————— No. 3, in E flat major (Peters)
—————— No. 4, in A major (Peters)

———— No. 5, in D major (Peters)
Novak, V.—Op. 7, in C minor (Universal)
Pfeiffer—Op. 119, in F (Augener)
Pleyel—Op. 44. (3 parts) (easy) (Augener)
———— Op. 48. *Six Sonatas* (Augener)
Prout—Op. 18, in F (Augener)
Raff, J.—Op. 202. (No. 1, in G major, and No. 2, in C minor)
Reinecke, C.—Op. 272 (easy)
Rheinberger, J.—Op. 38, in E flat (Siegel, Leipzig)
Rheinhold, H.—Op. 5, in B flat (Steing)
Saint-Saëns—Op. 41, in B flat
Scharwenka—Op. 37, in F major
Schumann, G.—Op. 29, in F minor (Universal)
Schumann, R.—Op. 47, in E flat major (one of the finest)
    (Peters)
Schütt—Op. 12, in F major
Squire, W. H.—*Serenade* (2 violins, cello, and piano) (Augener)
Strauss, R.—Op. 13, in C minor
Weber—Op. 8, in B flat major (Peters)

PIANO QUINTETS
(PIANO AND STRING QUARTET UNLESS OTHERWISE NOTED)

Arensky—Op. 51 (Jurgensen)
Beethoven—Op. 16, in E flat (oboe, clarinet, horn, and bassoon)
Brahms—Op. 34, in F minor (Universal)
D'Indy—Op. 81 (Senart)
Dóhnanyi—Op. 26, in E flat major
Dubois, T.—*Quintet in F Major* (violin, oboe (clarinet), cello and viola) (Durand)
Dvořák—Op. 81, in A major
Fauré, G.—Op. 89, in D minor
———— Op. 115, in C minor (Durand)
Fibich—Op. 42 (violin, clarinet, horn, cello, and piano)
Foote, A.—Op. 38, in A minor
Franck,—*Quintet in F Minor* (Hamelle)
Giannini, V.—*Quintet* (Schirmer)
Goldmark—Op. 30, in B flat major (Universal)

Grunberg, L.—Op. 38.
Herzogenberg—Op. 48 (oboe, clarinet, horn, bassoon, and piano)
Holbrooke, J.—Op. 44, in G minor (Chester)
Jadassohn—Op. 70. *First Quintet*
——— Op. 76, in F major (melodious)
Juon—Op. 38 (violin, 2 violas, cello, and piano)
——— Op. 44, in F major
Labor—Op. 11 (clarinet, violin, viola, cello, and piano) (Universal)
Lacombe—Op. 26, in F sharp minor (violin, oboe, cello, bassoon, and piano)
Mozart—*Quintet* (oboe, clarinet, horn, bassoon, and piano)
Pleyel—Op. 8. *Six Easy Quintets* (Augener)
Prout—Op. 3 (Augener)
Reger—Op. 64, in C minor
Rheinberger—Op. 114, in C major
Rimski-Korsakov—*Quintet in B Flat* (flute, clarinet, horn, and bass) (Jurgensen)
Saint George—*Petite Suite* (easy) (Augener)
Saint-Saëns—Op. 14, in A minor (Hamelle)
Schubert—Op. 114 (violin, viola, cello, bass, and piano)
Schumann, G.—Op. 18
Schumann, R.—Op. 44, in E flat (Peters)
Sgambati—Op. 4, in F minor (Schott)
Sinding, C.—Op. 5, in E minor
Tcherepnin—Op. 44 (solo viola & piano) (A.M.P.)
Turina, J.—*Piano Quintet* (Spanish qualities) (Mathot)
——— *Scene Andalouse* (string quartet)
Widor—Op. 68
Wolff-Ferrari—Op. 6, in D flat (Schott)

SEXTETS WITH PIANO

Bennett, W. S.—Op. 8. *Piano Sextet* (Augener)
Jadassohn—Op. 100 (piano, 4 hands, and string quartet)
Juon, Paul—Op. 22 (2 violins, viola, 2 cellos, and piano)
——— Op. 51. *Divertimenti* (flute, oboe, clarinet, bassoon, and piano) (Schlesinger)
Mendelssohn—Op. 110 (2 violins, viola, cello, double bass, piano)

Pick-Mangiagalli—Op. 4. *Miniatures* (piano and string quintet)
Quef, C.—*Suite* (flute, oboe, clarinet, horn, bassoon, and piano)
Rheinberger—Op. 191 (flute, oboe, clarinet, bassoon, horn, and piano)
Weber—Op. 35, in E flat (2 violins, horn, viola, cello, and piano)
Woss—Op. 46, in E minor (2 violins, viola, cello, bass or 2nd cello, and piano)

SEPTETS WITH PIANO

Duvernoy—*Serenade* (2 violins, viola, cello, D bass, trumpet, piano)
Hummel—Op. 74 (flute, oboe, horn, viola, cello, bass, piano)
Saint-Saëns—Op. 65 (2 violins, viola, cello, D bass, trumpet, piano)
Spohr—Op. 147, in A minor, (violin, cello, flute, clarinet, horn, bassoon, piano)
Steinbach—Op. 7, in A major (oboe, clarinet, horn, violin, viola, cello, piano)

OCTETS WITH PIANO

Dolmetsch—Op. 29 (violin, alto, cello, bass, flute, clarinet, horn, piano)
Rubinstein, A.—Op. 9 (violin, alto, cello, bass, flute, clarinet, horn, piano)

NONETS WITH PIANO

Czerny—Op. 95. *Nocturne* (flute, clarinet, horn, bassoon, violin, alto, cello, bass, piano)
Wolff-Ferrari—Op. 8. *Kammer Symphonie* (flute, clarinet, oboe, bassoon, horn, 2 violins, viola, cello, D bass, and piano)

BOOKS ON MUSICAL SUBJECTS

Annesley, Charles.—*Home Book of the Operas*. New York: Tudor Publishing Co.

Baker, Theodore.—*Dictionary of Musical Terms.* New York: G. Schirmer.

——— *A Pronouncing Manual of Musical Terms.* New York: Charles Scribner's Sons.

——— *Biographical Dictionary of Musicians.* New York: G. Schirmer.

Baltzell, Winto James.—*A Complete History of Music for Schools.*

Bekker, Paul.—*The Story of Music.* New York: W. W. Norton & Co.

Bernstein, Martin.—*Introduction to Music.* New York: Prentice-Hall, Inc.

Brower, Harriette.—*Piano Mastery.* 2 vols. New York: Frederick A. Stokes Co.

——— *Self Help in Piano Study.* New York: Frederick A. Stokes Co.

——— *What to Play; What to Teach.* Philadelphia: The Theo. Presser Co.

——— *Life Stories of Master Musicians.* Philadelphia: The Theo. Presser Co.

——— *Modern Masters of the Keyboard.* New York: Frederick A. Stokes Co.

Buonamici, Carlo.—*Practical Hints on Piano Playing.* Boston: O. Ditson & Co.

Burrowes, John Freckleton.—*The Pianoforte Primer.* New York: G. Schirmer.

Busoni, Ferruccio.—*Sketch of a New Esthetic of Music.* New York: G. Schirmer.

Buzzi-Peccia, A.—*How to Succeed in Singing.* Philadelphia: The Theo. Presser Co.

Calvocoressi & Abraham. *Biographical Studies of Russian Composers.* New York: Alfred A. Knopf, Inc.

Clarke, Hugh, A.—*Pronouncing Musical Dictionary.* Philadelphia: The Theo. Presser Co.

Clifford, J. H.—*The Music Lover's Handbook.* New York: University Society.

Cooke, James Francis.—*Great Pianists on Piano Playing.*

Copland, Aaron.—*What to Listen For in Music.* New York: Whittlesey House.

Coward, Henry.—*Choral Technique and Interpretation.* New York: H. W. Gray, Inc.

Dannreuther, Edward.—*Richard Wagner and the Reform of Opera*. London: Augener & Co.

Dickinson, Clarence.—*Excursions in Musical History*. New York: H. W. Gray, Inc.

Dickinson, Edward.—*The Education of a Music Lover*. New York: Charles Scribner's Sons.

———— *Students Book of Inspiration*. Boston: Houghton Mifflin Co.

———— *The Study of the History of Music*. New York: Charles Scribner's Sons.

———— *The Spirit of Music*.

———— *Music and the Higher Education*.

———— *Music in the History of the Western Church*.

D'Indy, Vincent.—*Beethoven*. Boston: Boston Music Co.

Downes, Olin.—*Symphonic Masterpieces*. New York: Tudor Publishing Co.

Ehrenfechter.—*Delivery in the Art of Piano Playing*. London: Reeves Co.

Ehrlich, A.—*How to Practice the Piano*. New York: G. Schirmer.

———— *Celebrated Pianists of the Past and Present Time*. Leipzig: A. H. Payne.

Ekman, Karl.—*Jean Sibelius*. New York: Alfred A. Knopf, Inc.

Elson, Arthur.—*The Book of Musical Knowledge*. New York: Halcyon House.

Elterlein, Ernst von.—*Beethoven's Sonatas*. New York: Charles Scribner's Sons.

Engel, Karl.—*Alla Breve, from Bach to Debussy*.

Erb, J. Lawrence.—*Musical Appreciation for the Student*.

Erskine, John.—*The Philharmonic Symphony Society of New York*. New York: The Macmillan Co.

Farrar, Geraldine.—*Such Sweet Compulsion*. New York: The Greystone Press.

Finck, Henry T.—*Musical Progress*.

Flower.—*Franz Schubert, the Man and his Circle*. New York: Tudor Publishing Co.

Forsyth, Cecil.—*Orchestration*. New York: The Macmillan Co.

Gantvoort, Arnold J.—*Familiar Talks on the History of Music*.

Gehrkens, C.—*Musical Notation: Terminology*. New York: A. S. Barnes Co.

——— *Handbook of Musical Terms*. Boston: O. Ditson & Co.

——— *Handbook of Conducting*.

Grabbe, Paul.—*For the Music Lover: Stories of 100 Operas*.

Hamilton, C. G.—*Outlines of Musical History*. Boston: O. Ditson & Co.

——— *Ornaments in Classical and Modern Music*. Boston: O. Ditson & Co.

——— *Epochs in Musical Progress*. Boston: O. Ditson & Co.

——— *Piano Music, Composers and Characteristics*. Boston: O. Ditson & Co.

Harding, Henry A.—*Analysis of Form*. New York: H. W. Gray, Inc.

Hargrave, Mary.—*The Earlier French Musicians*. New York: E. P. Dutton & Co., Inc.

Harrison.—*Music for the Multitude*. New York: The Macmillan Co.

Heacox, A. E.—*Keyboard Training in Harmony*. New York and Leipzig: Schmidt & Co.

——— *Harmony for Ear, Eye and Keyboard*. Boston: O. Ditson & Co.

——— *Lessons in Harmony*. Oberlin, Ohio: A. G. Comings & Sons.

——— *Project Lessons in Orchestration*. Boston: O. Ditson & Co.

Hipkins, Alfred James.—*Ancient Musical Instruments*. London: A. & C. Black.

——— *A Description and History of the Pianoforte*. New York: H. W. Gray, Inc.

Howard, J. Tasker.—*Stephen Foster*. New York: Tudor Publishing Co.

Hubbard, W. Z.—*Operas*. 2 vols. New York: Irving Squire.

Hughes, R. and Deems Taylor.—*Music Lovers' Encyclopedia*. New York: Garden City Publishing Co.

Isaacson, Charles D.—*Face to Face with Great Musicians*. New York: Boni & Liveright.

Istel, Edgar.—*The Art of Writing Opera Librettos*.

Kelley, Edgar Stillman.—*The Orchestral Instruments*.

——— *Chopin, the Composer*.

Kleczynski, J.—*How to Play Chopin*. London: Reeves & Co.

Klein, Herman.—*Thirty Years of Musical Life in London.* New York: The Century Co.

Krehbiel, H. E.—*First Book of Opera Plots.* New York: The Macmillan Co.

———— *Second Book of Opera Plots.* New York: The Macmillan Co.

———— *How to Listen to Music.* New York: Charles Scribner's Sons.

Kullak, Franz.—*Beethoven's Piano Playing.* New York: G. Schirmer.

Lahee, Henry.—*Famous Pianists.* Boston: L. C. Page Co.

Langhans, William.—*The History of Music.* New York: G. Schirmer.

Le Couppey, Felix.—*Piano Teaching.* Philadelphia: Theo. Presser Co.

Lehmann, J. F.—*Form in Music.*

———— *The Analysis of Form in Music.* Oberlin, Ohio: A. G. Comings & Sons.

———— *Simple Counterpoint.*

Lenz, Wilhelm von.—*The Great Piano Virtuosos of Our Time.* New York: G. Schirmer.

Lewis, Leon Rich.—*The Ambitious Listener.* Boston: O. Ditson & Co.

Lhevinne, Joseph.—*Basic Principles of Piano Playing.* Philadelphia: The Theo. Presser Co.

Lillie, Lucy.—*The Story of Music and Musicians.* New York: Harper & Brothers.

Lindo, A. H.—*The Art of Accompanying.* New York: G. Schirmer.

———— *A Neglected Sense in Piano Playing.* New York: G. Schirmer.

Macklin, C. B.—*Elementary Pedagogy.* Philadelphia: The Theo. Presser Co.

Martens, Fred H.—*The Art of the Prima Donna.* New York: D. Appleton and Co.

One Thousand and One Nights of Opera. New York: D. Appleton and Co.

Mason, Daniel Gregory.—*The Orchestral Instruments and What They Do.* New York: H. W. Gray, Inc.

———— *Music in My Time and Other Reminiscences.* New York: The Macmillan Co.

Matthay, Tobias.—*Musical Interpretation.* Boston: Boston Music Co.

Mayrott, Harold.—*Musical Essentials.* Church & Co.

McSpaddin, J. W.—*Opera Synopses.* London: Geo. Harrap.

——— *Stories from Wagner.* London: Geo. Harrap.

Melitz, Leo.—*The Opera-Goer's Complete Guide.* New York: Garden City Publishing Co.

Moscheles, Ignaz.—*Recent Music and Musicians.* New York: Henry Holt & Co., Inc.

Neumann, Angelo.—*Personal Recollections of Richard Wagner.*

Newmarch, Rosa.—*The Concert-Goer's Library of Descriptive Notes.* 6 vols. (Explanations of practically every orchestral composition heard in concerts). New York: Oxford University Press.

——— *The Life and Letters of Tchaikovski.* London and New York: John Lane Co.

Parker, D. C.—*A Study of Percy Grainger.* New York: G. Schirmer.

Pirro, André.—*Johann Sebastian Bach.* New York: G. Schirmer.

Polko, Elise.—*Musical Sketches.* New York: Sturgis, Walton & Co.

Potocka, Countess. *Theodore Leschitizky.*

Pratt, Waldo S.—*New Encyclopedia of Music.* New York: The Macmillan Co.

——— *The History of Music.* New York: G. Schirmer.

Prunieres, Henri.—*A New History of Music.* New York: The Macmillan Co.

Pulyer, Jeff.—*A Dictionary of Old English Music.* New York: E. P. Dutton & Co., Inc.

Redfield.—*Music.* New York: Tudor Publishing Co.

Rimsky-Korsakoff, Nikolai.—*My Musical Life.* New York: Tudor Publishing Co.

Rogers, Francis.—*Some Famous Singers of the Nineteenth Century.* New York: H. W. Gray, Inc.

Rolland, Romain.—*Life of Beethoven.*

Rosenfield, Hugo—*Musical Portraits.* New York: Harcourt, Brace & Co., Inc.

Schinn, Frederick—*Musical Theory and Its Cultivation.* Boston: O. Ditson & Co.

Seymore, H. A.—*How to Think Music.* New York: G. Schirmer.

Smith, Hannah—*Founders of Music.* New York: G. Schirmer.

Sonneck, O. G.—*Miscellaneous Studies in the History of Music.* New York: G. Schirmer.

———— *Early Opera in America.* New York: G. Schirmer.

———— *Suum Cuique.* (Essays). New York: G. Schirmer.

———— *Beethoven: Impressions of Contemporaries.* New York: G. Schirmer.

———— *The Riddle of the Immortal Beloved.* New York: G. Schirmer.

Spaeth, Sigmund.—*Great Program Music: How to Enjoy and Remember It.* New York: Garden City Publishing Co.

Stefan, Paul.—*Anton Dvorak: His Life and Work.* New York: The Greystone Press.

Sternberg, Constantin.—*Tempo Rubato.* New York: G. Schirmer.

———— *The Ethics and Esthetics of Piano Playing.* New York: G. Schirmer.

Stoeving, Paul—*The Violin: Its Makers and Players.* Boston: O. Ditson & Co.

Strong, L. A. G.—*John McCormack,* New York: The Macmillan Co.

Swisher, Walter, S.—*Psychology for the Music Teacher.* Boston: O. Ditson & Co.

———— *Music in Worship.* Boston: O. Ditson & Co.

Thayer, Alexander W.—*The Life of Beethoven.* New York: G. Schirmer.

Upton, George P.—*Standard Operas.* Chicago: A. C. McClurg & Co.

———— *Standard Concert Repertory.* Chicago: A. C. McClurg & Co.

———— *Standard Musical Biographies.* Chicago: A. C. McClurg & Co.

———— *Woman in Music.* Chicago: A. C. McClurg & Co.

Upton, W. T.—*The Art Song in America.* Boston: O. Ditson & Co.

Vining, H. C.—*The Simple and Complete Primer for the Pianoforte.* New York: G. Schirmer.

Watkins, Mary Fitch.—*Behind the Scenes at the Opera*. New York: Frederick A. Stokes Co.

——— *First Aid to the Opera-Goer*. New York: Frederick A. Stokes Co.

Wedge, George A.—*Rhythm in Music*.

White, Robert T.—*The Teaching of Music*. New York: G. Schirmer.

——— *Playing at Sight*. London: Curwen & Sons.

Wier.—*The Piano*. New York: Longmans, Green & Co.

MUSIC NOVELS AND LIVES OF MUSICIANS

Atherton, Gertrude.—*The Tower of Ivory*. New York: The Macmillan Co. (Wagner at Munich)

Bacon, Dolores M.—*The Diary of a Musician*. New York: Henry Holt & Co., Inc.

Bercovici, Konrad.—*For a Song*. New York: Dodd, Mead & Co., Inc.

Bromfield, Louis.—*Possession*.

Buhrman, T. Scott.—*Bach's Life Chronologically*. New York: Organ Interests, Inc.

Chotzinoff, Samuel.—*Eroica*. New York: Simon & Schuster. (Beethoven's Life)

Damrosch, Walter. *My Musical Life*. New York: Charles Scribner's Sons.

Davenport, Marcia.—*Of Lena Geyer*. New York: Charles Scribner's Sons.

Day, Lillian.—*Paganini of Genoa*. New York: The Macaulay Co.

Draper, Muriel.—*Music at Midnight*. New York: Harper & Brothers.

Godfrey, Elizabeth.—*Poor Human Nature*. New York: Henry Holt & Co. Inc. (Wagnerian tenor)

Harraden, Beatrice.—*Patuffa*. New York: Frederick A. Stokes Co. (violinist)

Haweis, H. R.—*My Musical Memories*. New York: Funk & Wagnalls Co.

Kennedy, Margaret.—*The Constant Nymph*. New York: Doubleday & Co. (composer's family)

Kobbe, Gustave.—*All of a Sudden Carmen*. New York: G. P. Putnam's Sons.

Moore, George.—*Evelyn Innes.* New York: D. Appleton & Co.

Nordling, Johan.—*The Moonlight Sonata.* New York: Sturgis, Walton & Co. (Beethoven)

Pourtales, Guy de.—*Franz Liszt.* New York: Henry Holt & Co. Inc.

Reed, Myrtle. *The Master's Violin.* New York: G. P. Putnam's Sons

Roberts, Cecil.—*The Love Rack.* New York: Frederick A. Stokes Co. (violinist)

Rolland, Romain.—*Goethe and Beethoven.* New York: Harper & Brothers.

———— *Jean Christophe.* New York: Henry Holt & Co., Inc.

———— *Beethoven the Creator.* New York: Henry Holt & Co., Inc.

Runkel, Bertha.—*The Truth about Tolna.* New York: The Century Co. (mysterious tenor)

Sanborn, Pitts.—*The Prima Donna.* 2 vols. New York: Longmans, Green & Co.

Schmidt, Carl.—*Notturno.* Philadelphia: The Theo. Presser Co.

Sedgwick, Anne Douglas. *Tante.* New York: The Century Co. (pianist)

Strachey, Marjory.—*The Nightingale.* New York: Longmans, Green & Co. (Chopin)

Werfel, Franz.—*Verdi.* New York: Simon & Schuster. (Verdi and Wagner in Venice)

Wolzogen, Ernst von.—*Florian Mayr.* New York: B. W. Huebsch & Co.